Instructor's Manual
to Accompany

Your Guide to Getting Fit

THIRD EDITION

Ivan Kusinitz
York College, City University of New York

Morton Fine
York College, City University of New York

Mayfield Publishing Company
Mountain View, California
London • Toronto

Copyright © 1995, 1991, 1987 by Mayfield Publishing Company

All rights reserved. No portion of this book may be reproduced in any form or by any means without written permission of the publisher.

International Standard Book Number: 1-55934-381-8

Manufactured in the United States of America
10 9 8 7 6 5 4 3 2 1

Mayfield Publishing Company
1280 Villa Street
Mountain View, California 94041

TABLE OF CONTENTS

Introduction: The College Fitness Course	v
Chapter Overviews, Tips, and References	
Chapter 1: How Fit Are You?	1
Chapter 2: Physical Fitness Training Principles	7
Chapter 3: Cardiorespiratory Endurance	9
Chapter 4: Body Composition	15
Chapter 5: Muscular Strength, Muscular Endurance, and Flexibility	20
Chapter 6: Model Exercise Programs and Appendix B	26
Chapter 7: Getting Started and Keeping Going	30
Chapter 8: Eating Right	32
Chapter 9: Model Weight Management Program	36
Chapter 10: Managing Stress	39
Chapters 11, 12, and 13: Exercising at Home or at a Fitness Facility, Programs for Special Needs, and Common Training Questions Answered	41
Lab Worksheets	45
Fitness Profiles	70
Examination Questions	109
Transparency Masters	

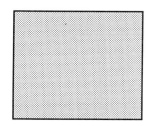

Introduction: The College Fitness Course

Although many colleges and universities have included basic fitness courses in their offerings for many years, the recent advent of the fitness boom has compelled most colleges and students to recognize fitness as an essential component of a broad education.

Some schools include the fitness experience as a basic curriculum requirement, while others provide the fitness course on an elective basis. Either way, a growing demand exists for well-organized courses designed to satisfy student fitness needs.

The Purpose of the Fitness Course

It would be ideal if, at the completion of a fitness course, all students enjoyed a high level of fitness and were motivated to maintain that level throughout their lives. It is more realistic, however, in light of the time usually allotted for fitness courses, for the goals of the course to be somewhat limited.

In the traditional 30- or 45-hour course extending over a 15-week period, students rarely become expert in the "whys" of exercise and fitness, become highly fit, and also develop the attitude needed to guarantee ongoing compliance with an exercise regimen.

We believe that a typical college fitness course is successful if, as a result, students can plan and follow a personal fitness program based on the selection of their own goals and activities.

To achieve this purpose, students need a process that guides them through program development choices and decisions, orchestrates academic and laboratory experiences, and fosters a commitment to fitness outside of class so that they can make exercise an integral part of their lifestyles.

Course Organization

Facts about exercise are an important ingredient in a fitness course, but their presentation should be kept in perspective and viewed as part of a system to achieve a broader purpose. If possible, class sessions that use the lecture or discussion approach to disseminate information should be limited to what is essential to get students started and keep them going on their exercise program.

Unfortunately, instructors often do not have control of how courses are scheduled. The time allocations, as well as the specific availability of laboratory and lecture sessions, are often determined by the administration; where the scheduling pattern provides for lectures only, the fitness profiles, lab worksheets, and exercises can be done by students on their own time.

When possible, however, a series of introductory sessions should provide a base of information and give direction to the program development process. Didactic sessions may be reduced or even discontinued after a few weeks, with the primary focus thereafter on the labs and on small group work or individual monitoring of progress.

Specifically, the lecture portions of the course can present background information leading to an understanding of fitness while at the same time preparing students for the laboratory sessions. The laboratory sessions in the gymnasium or exercise facility can provide opportunities for fitness testing, student experimentation with model programs, and fulfilling contract commitments.

We have had many years of experience with a system that allowed students to schedule their lecture and lab sessions separately. With this approach, the lecture classes accommodate large numbers of students and meet for up to two hours each week for half the term. An appropriate number of lab sections are scheduled to satisfy the number of students enrolled in the lecture. Each lab section meets twice weekly for one hour throughout the semester and is limited to an enrollment of 40 students. Lecture and lab sections are coordinated to facilitate the flow of subject matter and lab experiences.

Fitness Counselors

A critical element in the course is monitoring student progress, a task that can be particularly unwieldy when dealing with large numbers of students. We have found the use of trained student fitness counselors to be invaluable in helping to individualize the course. Fitness counselors are selected from among students who have successfully completed the course. The fitness counselor's functions within the lab include the following:

- to monitor the program development and implementation process of individual students and to serve as an advisor when necessary
- to assist with fitness testing
- to guide student use of equipment
- to conduct small group sessions dealing with specific laboratory experiences
- to help teach model programs

The Materials

The Instructor's Manual provides full-page copies of all the fitness profiles, lab worksheets, overhead transparency masters, and test questions.

The Chapter Guides

Chapter guides include an introductory overview that suggests how the instructor might present the materials. The instructor is free to pick and choose from the content summary ideas listed beside each of the chapter objectives. In addition, the appropriate transparency masters, lab worksheets, and fitness profiles that can be helpful in presenting the materials are listed.

The Lab Worksheets

The lab worksheets are written tasks, organized by chapter, for students to do on their own in preparation for the lecture-discussion and laboratory sessions. They are designed to be submitted to the instructor and can serve as an excellent vehicle for determining whether specific chapter objectives have been achieved. They provide an opportunity for instructor-student communication and feedback and can be particularly useful in situations with large numbers of students and limited potential for instructor-student interaction.

The Fitness Profiles

Fitness profile masters are included in this manual to allow the instructor the flexibility for duplication and distribution. In addition, the fitness profiles can be used for bulletin-board display.

Overhead Transparency Masters

Full-page overhead transparency masters are sequentially arranged for use as desired within the lecture-discussion sessions. These masters consist of illustrations, tables, charts, and content summaries. The pages can be removed and converted into acetate transparencies using copying machines that are available in most schools. These transparencies can be used on overhead projectors to visually present ideas and summarize subject matter. They are an excellent vehicle for the introduction, clarification, and clinching of concepts.

Test Questions

True/false and multiple-choice test questions, organized by chapter, are available to add to the instructor's bank of assessment materials.

Evaluation and Grades

Student evaluation should be based on the achievement of the course goal and its specific objectives. While a grading system is most prevalent, some institutions use a pass/fail approach. Lab worksheet and fitness profile completion, coupled with written examinations, pre- and post-fitness testing, and instructor observation of class participation, can provide adequate data for student assessment and evaluation.

A Note to the Instructor

Preparations before the semester:

- Review the chapter guides for ease in preparing your lectures.
- Make an ample number of copies of the laboratory worksheets and fitness profiles.
- Use the overhead transparency masters to make acetate transparencies for projection during specific lectures.
- Organize your materials by lecture as recommended in the chapter guides.

During the semester:

- Distribute laboratory worksheets for completion by students. Evaluate and return. These may be assigned so that students can prepare for each lecture. Some instructors assign these as summaries of the lecture.
- Distribute fitness profiles if you plan to collect and review them. Otherwise, have students complete them in the textbook.
- Use the overhead transparency masters to help illustrate your lectures.

How Fit Are You?

Seven transparencies can be used to clarify chapter content during a lecture-discussion. Two lab worksheets can be used to prepare students for the lecture-discussions or can serve afterwards as reinforcement. Fitness Profiles 1-1 through 1-9 guide students through fitness assessment and goal setting. Specific suggestions for fitness testing are provided. Two or three lab sessions should be adequate to test the entire class.

OVERVIEW

OBJECTIVE	CONTENT SUMMARY	TRANSP.	LAB WKSHT.	PROFILE
Define fitness.	Fitness implies a spectrum of functions: • carry out daily tasks without fatigue • ample energy for leisure-time pursuits • handle occasional unexpected emergencies	1		
Identify place on fitness continuum.	The full spectrum of physical fitness can be viewed as a continuum.	2	1-1	
Decide on medical clearance.	It is generally safe to begin an exercise program if you are under thirty-five, have no physical complaints, and have had a medical checkup within the past two years.	3	1-1	
Assess your activity level.	You can estimate your current level of activity by completing Fitness Profile 1-1.	4	1-1	1-1

1

OBJECTIVE	CONTENT SUMMARY	TRANSP.	LAB WKSHT.	PROFILE
	Your activity index will help to determine which of five activity patterns you fit into.			
	Your activity index can also help determine your readiness to increase your activity level and to take all of the fitness tests.			
Define the five fitness components.	Health-related physical fitness consists of five components, each separately defined.	5	1-2	
	Activities vary in their potential to influence the development of each of the five components.			
Assess physical fitness.	Fitness Profiles 1-2 through 1-8 help you to assess your physical fitness in terms of each of the five components.	6	1-2	1-2 to 1-9
	For testing suggestions, see below: "Assessing Physical Fitness — Your Fitness Profiles 1-2 to 1-9."			
Identify goals and components involved.	Fitness goals require that you upgrade one or more fitness components.	7	1-2	
	Upgrading your status in any component helps to achieve many goals.			

Assessing Physical Fitness — Your Fitness Profiles 1-2 to 1-9

Identifying personal fitness levels early in the course provides a basis for establishing personal fitness goals. In addition, gathering such baseline data is the first step in measuring individual progress when the same tests are repeated at the conclusion of the course.

It is best if personal fitness assessment is completed within the first several sessions. There are numerous ways of organizing the testing program, depending on how your course is set up. In any case it is helpful to place testing or lab stations around your facility. It is recommended that you assign trained "fitness counselors" or graduate assistants to each of the stations. Their roles will differ, depending on the nature and requirements of each of the tests. When possible, the students themselves should complete their own testing assisted by a student partner; and, of course, they should individually complete Fitness Profiles 1-2 through 1-9.

We recommend that copies be made of each profile from the masters in this instructor's manual, so that students need not tear pages from the text.

Suggestions for each of the test items follow:

FITNESS PROFILE 1-2: Taking the Modified Step Test

Preparation

It is helpful to prepare an audiocassette tape containing specific instructions.

a. Brief introduction to test
b. Signal to "GET READY"
c. Signal to "BEGIN"
d. Provide correct cadence "UP AND DOWN AND, etc." (continue for three minutes and intersperse with cues and encouragement such as: "TIME LEFT...", "DOING GREAT", etc.).
e. At end of 3 minutes, instruction should be "UP AND DOWN AND SIT."
f. At 45 seconds of rest, give signal to "GET READY TO COUNT PULSE."
g. At 60 seconds, give signal to "COUNT."
h. At 30 seconds of counting, give signal to "STOP."

Equipment and Materials

- Enough 8" step-up benches to facilitate testing
- A chair for each person to be tested at testing station
- Audiocassette player and instruction tape
- Pencils
- A copy of Fitness Profile 1-2 for each student
- If you don't have an instruction tape, you will need to provide a metronome and a stopwatch.

Tips

- Divide class into groups of two — have one tested by the other, then switch.
- Have five groups test themselves at one time (thus ten students will have been tested within approximately 10 minutes).
- If a tape isn't made, a student timer will be needed.

FITNESS PROFILE 1-3: Taking the 1.5-Mile Run-Walk Test

Preparation

- Mark course or track at 1.5 miles — six laps on a quarter-mile track equal 1.5 miles.
- Have someone call out times as students cross finish line, or place a large clock with a sweep second hand at the finish line.

Equipment and Materials

- Stopwatch or clock with sweep second hand
- A copy of Fitness Profile 1-3 for each student
- Pencils

Tips

- Have 8 or 10 (or more) students start together.
- Starter can serve as timer on a quarter-mile track.
- Be sure students warm up before the test and walk a lap afterwards.
- Students who have been sedentary should not be tested until later in the course (see page 11 in the text).

FITNESS PROFILE 1-4: Determining Your Body Build

Preparation

Provide a copy of this profile for each student, and suggest that the students complete this profile at home.

FITNESS PROFILE 1-5: Methods for Assessing Body Composition

Using Skinfold Calipers

Preparation

- Train "fitness counselors," graduate assistants or other students to use skinfold calipers.

Equipment and Materials

- Enough calipers to facilitate testing
- Privacy screens if desired
- A copy of Fitness Profile 1-5 for each student
- "Percent of body fat" charts at testing stations
- Rulers

Tips

- Have students use the charts to estimate their own percent of body fat.

Using the Body Mass Index

Preparation

- Suggest that students do this at home.

FITNESS PROFILE 1-6: Taking the Grip-Strength Dynamometer Test

Preparation

- Have a trained student supervise this station.

Equipment and Materials

- Enough hand dynamometers to facilitate testing
- A copy of Fitness Profile 1-6 for each student

FITNESS PROFILE 1-7: Testing Muscular Endurance

Preparation

- Set up two stations, one for the 60-second sit-up and one for the push-up.
- Train a student timer for the 60-second sit-up.

Equipment and Materials

- One stopwatch for the sit-up test
- A copy of Fitness Profile 1-7 for each student

Tips

- Students should work in pairs.
- One starter can call the time for as many as half a class of students at one time.
- A similar approach can be used with the push-up test but without any timing.

FITNESS PROFILE 1-8: Trunk Flexibility

Preparation

- Prepare the testing boxes as described in Fitness Profile 1-8.

Equipment and Materials

- Enough boxes with rulers to facilitate testing
- A copy of Fitness Profile 1-8 for each student

Tips

- It is helpful if students work in pairs; one performs while one reads and records.

References

American Alliance for Health, Physical Education, Recreation and Dance. *Lifetime Health - Related Physical Fitness*. Reston, VA: AAHPERD, 1980.

American College of Sports Medicine. *Guidelines for Exercise Testing and Prescription*. Philadelphia: Lea and Febiger, 1986.

American Heart Association. *Exercise Testing and Training of Apparently Healthy Individuals: A Handbook for Physicians*. New York: AHA, 1972.

Bloom, M. "Fitness in America: Is Medicine Keeping Up?" *Medical World News* (November 1978): 66.

Cooper, K., et al. "Physical Fitness Levels vs. Selected Coronary Risk Factors." *Journal of the American Medical Association* 236, no. 2 (1976): 166.

Golding, L. A., C. R. Myers, and W. E. Sinning. *Y's Way to Physical Fitness*. Champaign, IL: Human Kinetics Pub., 1989.

Harris, L., and Associates. *The Perrier Study: Fitness in America*. New York: Great Waters of France, 1979.

Haskell, W. L., H. J. Montoye, and D. Orenstein. "Physical Activity and Exercise to Achieve Health-Related Physical Fitness Components." *Public Health Rep.* 100: (1985): 202–212.

Kannel, W., and P. Sorlie, "Some Health Benefits of Physical Activity. The Framingham Study." *Archives of Internal Medicine* 139 (1979): 857-61.

Katch, F. I., and W. D. McArdle. *Nutrition, Weight Control, and Exercise*. Philadelphia: Lea and Febiger, 1983.

Kennedy, J. F. "The Soft American." *Sports Illustrated* 13 (December 1960): 15.

Lamb, L. E. "How Fat Are You?" *The Health Letter* 27, no. 6 (1986): 1-2.

Montoye, H. J., et al. "Heart Rate Response to a Modified Harvard Step Test: Males and Females, age 10-69." *Research Quarterly* 40, no. 1.

Osternig, L. R. "Isokinetic Dynamometry: Implications for Muscle Testing and Rehabilitation." *Exercise and Sport Sciences Reviews* 14 (1986): 45–80.

Pollock, M. L., J. H. Wilmore, and S. M. Fox. *Health and Fitness through Physical Activity*. New York: John Wiley and Sons, 1978.

Pollock, M. L., and J. H. Wilmore. *Exercise in Health and Disease: Evaluation and Prescription for Prevention and Rehabilitation*. 2nd ed. Philadelphia: W.B. Saunders, 1990.

Thompson, P. D. "The Safety of Exercise Testing and Participation," In: *Resource Manual for Guidelines for Exercise Testing and Participation*, S. N. Blair, P. Painter, R. R. Pate, L. K. Smith, and D. H. Taylor (eds.), 273-277. Philadelphia: Lea and Febiger, 1988.

U.S. Department of Health and Human Services. *The 1990 Health Objectives for the Nation: A Midcourse Review*. Washington: Government Printing Office. November 1986.

2

Physical Fitness Training Principles

This chapter is informational in nature; follow-up chapters contain applications of the training principles. The content can be clarified using the five transparencies during a lecture-discussion session. Lab Worksheet 2-1 can be assigned in preparation for the lecture-discussion or afterward for reinforcement.

OVERVIEW

OBJECTIVE	CONTENT SUMMARY	TRANSP.	LAB WKSHT.	PROFILE
Explain how progressive overload results in training effects.	Progressive overload is the gradual increase of demands on the body system, thus causing the body to mobilize its resources and become adapted to the increased workload. *Training effects* are the physiological adaptations resulting from progressive overload.	8	2-1	
Define intensity, duration, and frequency.	Intensity = how hard Duration = how long Frequency = how often	9	2-1	

OBJECTIVE	CONTENT SUMMARY	TRANSP.	LAB WKSHT.	PROFILE
Identify how the specific effects of an activity can achieve particular fitness goals.	The principle of specificity means that only those body systems stressed by an exercise program achieve the beneficial effects of fitness training.	10	2-1	
	For each fitness goal, a variety of activities exist that can provide the specificity to achieve desired training effects.			
	Using more than one activity to achieve a goal is called *cross-training*.	11		
Apply intensity, duration, and frequency of exercise to progressive overload.	Progressive overload is applied differently for each fitness component and may vary for different activities.	12	2-1	

References

American College of Sports Medicine. *Guidelines for Graded Exercise Testing and Exercise Prescription*. 3rd ed. Philadelphia: Lea and Febiger, 1986.

American College of Sports Medicine. "The Recommended Quantity and Quality of Exercise for Developing and Maintaining Cardiorespiratory and Muscular Fitness in Healthy Adults." *Medicine and Science in Sports and Exercise* 22, no. 2 (April 1990): 265–74.

Bompa, T. *Theory and Methodology of Training*. Dubuque, IA: Kendall/Hunt, 1985.

Coyle, E. F., W. H. Martin, D. R. Sinacore, M. J. Joyner, J. M. Hagberg, and J. O. Holloszy. "Time Course of Loss of Adaptation after Stopping Prolonged Intense Endurance Training." *Journal of Applied Physiology* 57 (1984): 1857–1864.

Fahey, T. D. (ed.). *Athletic Training: Principles and Practice*. Mountain View, CA: Mayfield Publishing, 1986.

Hickson, R.C., and M. A. Rosenkoetter. "Reduced Training Frequencies and Maintenance of Increased Aerobic Power." *Medicine and Science in Sports and Exercise* 13 (1981): 13.

Pollock, M. L., and S. N. Blair. "Exercise Prescription." *Journal of Physical Education and Recreation* 52 (1981): 30.

Pollock, M. L., et al. "Effects of Mode of Training on Cardiovascular Function and Body Composition of Adult Men." *Medicine and Science in Exercise and Sports* 7, no. 2 (1975): 139-45.

Pollock, M. L., et al. "Effects of Training Two Days Per Week at Different Intensities on Middle-aged Men." *Medical Science* 4 (1972): 192-97

Wilmore, J. H., and D. L. Costill. *Training for Sport and Activity. The Physiological Basis of the Conditioning Process*. 3rd ed. Dubuque, IA: Wm. C. Brown, 1988.

Cardiorespiratory Endurance

The basic information for understanding aerobic training can be presented during a single lecture-discussion. The transparencies provided will support such a presentation. The skill of monitoring heart rate (pulse counting) can be learned and mastered during a laboratory session. Lab Worksheet 3-1 can be assigned as preparation for the lecture-discussion or afterward as reinforcement.

OVERVIEW

OBJECTIVE	CONTENT SUMMARY	TRANSP.	LAB WKSHT.	PROFILE
Differentiate between aerobic and anaerobic activity.	An aerobic activity is any sustained, moderately strenuous effort at an intensity level just high enough for the heart and lungs to keep pace with the increased need for oxygen by the heart and other muscles.	13	3-1	
	An anaerobic activity requires an intense burst of muscular effort that outstrips the ability of the heart and lungs to keep up with the supply of oxygen needed. For several minutes after anaerobic activity has ended, the heart and lungs work overtime.	13		
	Examples of steady, rhythmic activities that are well-suited for aerobic development are: walking, jogging, swimming, bicycling, rowing, cross-country skiing, hiking, and rope skipping.	14		

OBJECTIVE	CONTENT SUMMARY	TRANSP.	LAB WKSHT.	PROFILE
Identify the training effects of aerobic activities and the role of exercise in heart health.	The size and strength of the heart muscle increases.	15	3-1	
	Heart rate at rest and during activity is reduced, but the amount of blood pumped during each heartbeat (stroke volume) and over one minute (cardiac output) is increased.	16		
	Time is reduced for the heart to return to resting levels.			
	In some people, resting blood pressure may be reduced.			
	HDL may be increased. This is the portion of blood cholesterol that may protect against coronary heart disease.			
	Blood may develop a decreased tendency to clot.			
Recognize the risk factors of coronary heart disease.	Some risk factors can be altered by making the right choices; others can't be changed.	17	3-1	
	Cholesterol levels can be a major risk factor.	18		
Determine the EBZ.	Intensity of aerobic activity determines its capacity to produce CRE training effects. Exercise intensity can be measured by counting heart rate during activity.		3-1	
	The Exercise Benefit Zone (EBZ) refers to the heart rate range intense enough to result in CRE training effects.	19		
	EBZ is determined by calculating the heart rate range between 60% and 85% of maximum heart rate. Maximum heart rate can be estimated by subtracting age from the figure 220.	20 22	3-1	

OBJECTIVE	CONTENT SUMMARY	TRANSP.	LAB WKSHT.	PROFILE
Measure heart rate.	Heart rate is easily measured by counting the pulse beats; either the radial or carotid artery can be used for this purpose. To estimate heart rate per minute, count your pulse for ten seconds and multiply by six.	21	3-1	
Determine exercise duration and frequency.	Duration of exercise period is limited when the intensity is high.		3-1	
	Self-paced activities lend themselves more readily to the control of intensity than do competitive sports. Therefore, duration is also better managed.	14 23		
	CRE improvement is facilitated when the aerobic activity is continued for 20 minutes or more within the EBZ.	23 24		
	Once a beginner becomes adjusted to exercise, duration can be increased by no more than 10% each week.			
	The recommended frequency of aerobic exercise for the beginner is three or four times per week.			
	Daily exercise, using the same activity each day, frequently leads to overuse injuries. If you require daily exercise, vary your activities.			
	Discontinuing a CRE program will result in deconditioning over a period of time.			
Recognize the relationship of calories used per week to various levels of CRE.	The term *calorie* (kilocalorie) refers to a unit of heat energy. The number of calories used in CRE activity for one week can be a useful measure of the intensity, duration, and frequency of a program.	25	3-1	

OBJECTIVE	CONTENT SUMMARY	TRANSP.	LAB WKSHT.	PROFILE
Identify how various training programs are used to develop CRE.	A simple and effective system for conducting CRE activity is the continuous rhythmic technique (CRT). This is activity at a slow and steady pace for an extended duration within the EBZ. While CRT may become boring for some, it is a system that is easy to master and to monitor. Interval training, a system that alternates high and low activity (or rest), enables the beginner to deal with limitations in CRE. The intervals of rest or low-intensity activity allow the body to partially recuperate from the higher-intensity work. Therefore, fatigue is delayed and a greater amount of work can be completed. Each complete interval of high and low activity is referred to as a *set*.		3-1	

References

American College of Sports Medicine. *Guidelines for Graded Exercise Testing and Exercise Prescription.* 3rd ed. Philadelphia: Lea and Febiger, 1986.

Blackburn, H., and D. R. Jacobs. "Physical Activity and the Risk of Coronary Heart Disease." In: *Proceedings of the Fifth World Congress on Cardiac Rehabilitation,* J. P. Boustet (ed.), 403–418. Hampshire, U.K.: Intercept, 1993.

Blair, S. N. "Physical Activity, Fitness, and Coronary Heart Disease." In: *Physical Activity, Fitness, and Health,* C. Bouchard, R. J. Shephard, and T. Stephens (eds.). Champaign, IL: Human Kinetics. (In press.)

Blair, S. N., N. N. Goodyear, L. W. Gibbons, and K. H. Cooper. "Physical Fitness and Incidence of Hypertension in Healthy Normotensive Men and Women." *Journal of the American Medical Association* 252 (1984): 487–90.

Blair, S. N., H. W. Kohl, N. F. Gordon, and R. S. Paffenbarger. "How Much Physical Activity is Good for Health?" *Annual Review of Public Health* 13 (1992): 99–126.

Blair, S. N., H. W. Kohl, III, R. S. Paffenbarger, D. G. Clark, K. H. Cooper, and L. H. Gibbons. "Physical Fitness and All-Cause Mortality. A Prospective Study of Healthy Men and Women." *Journal of the American Medical Association* 262 (1989): 2395–2401.

Blomqvist, C. G., and B. Saltin. "Cardiovascular Adaptations to Physical Training." *Annual Review of Physiology* 45 (1983): 169–189.

Bruce, R. "Primary Intervention against Coronary Atherosclerosis by Exercise Conditioning." *New England Journal of Mecicine* 305 (1981): 1525-6.

Bruce, R. A., K. F. Hossack, T. A. DeRouen, and V. Hofer. "Enhanced Risk Assessment for

Primary Coronary Heart Disease Events by Maximal Exercise Testing: 10 Years' Experience of Seattle Heart Watch." *Journal of American College Cardiology* 2(1983): 565–573.

Cooke, R., and Pate, E. "Inhibition of Muscle Contraction by the Products of ATP Hydrolysis, ADP, and Phosphate. *Biophysical Journal* 47 (1985): 25a.

Coplan, N. L., G. W. Gleim, and I. A. Nicholas. "Exercise and Sudden Cardiac Death." *American Heart Journal* 115(1 pt 1) (1988): 207–212.

Coyle, E. F., M. K. Hemmert, and A. W. Coggan. "Effects of Detraining on Cardiovascular Responses to Exercise: Role of Blood Volume." *Journal of Applied Physiology* 60 (1986): 95-99.

Crow, R., H. Blackburn, D. Jacobs, et al. "Population Strategies to Enhance Physical Activity: The Minnesota Heart Health Program." *Acta Medica Scandinavica Supplementum* 711 (1986): 93–112.

Fletcher, G. F., S. N. Blair, J. Blumenthal, C. Caspersen, B. Chaitman, S. Epstein, H. Falls, E. S. Sivarajan Froelicher, V. F. Froelicher, and I. L. Pina. "Statement on Exercise: Benefits and Recommendations for Physical Activity Programs for All Americans." *Circulation* 86 (1992): 340–344.

Gibson, H., and R. H. T. Edwards. "Muscular Exercise and Fatigue." *Sports Medicine* 2 (1985): 120–132.

Hagberg, J. M., J. E. Graves, M. Limacher, et al. "Cardiovascular Responses of 70–79 Year Old Men and Women to Exercise Training." *Journal of Applied Physiology* 66 (1989): 2589–2594.

Hickson, R. C., C. Foster, M. L. Pollock, T. M. Galassi, and S. Rich. "Reduced Training Intensities and Loss of Aerobic Power, Endurance, and Cardiac Growth. *Journal of Applied Physiology* 58 (1985): 492–499.

Holloszy, J. O. "Adaptation of Skeletal Muscle to Endurance Exercise," *Medical Science* 7, no. 3 (1975): 155–64.

Hopper, M. K., A. R. Coggan, and E. F. Coyle. "Exercise Stroke Volume Relative to Plasma-Volume Expansion." *Journal of Applied Physiology* 64 (1988): 404–408.

Jacobs, I., M. Esbjornsson, C. Sylven, I. Holm, and E. Jansson. "Sprint Training Effects on Muscle Myoglobin, Enzymes, Fiber Types, and Blood Lactate." *Medicine and Science in Sports and Exercise* 19 (1987): 368–74.

Joseph, J. J. "Effects of Calisthenics, Jogging and Swimming on Middle-Age Men," *Sports Medicine* (1974): 14.

Karvonen, M. J., et al. "Longevity of Endurance Skiers." *Medical Science* 6, no. 1 (1974): 59–51.

Kasch, F. W., and J. P. Wallace. "Physiological Variable During 10 Years of Endurance Exercise." *Medical Science* 8, no. 1 (1976): 5–8.

Lamb, L. E. "Update on Cholesterol and Triglycerides." *The Health Letter* 39, no. 7 (July 1992): 131-1–131-8.

Leon, A. S., J. Connett, D. R. Jacobs, and R. Rauramaa. "Leisure-time Activity Levels and Risk of Coronary Heart Disease and Death: The Multiple Risk of Coronary Heart Disease and Death: The Multiple Risk Factor Intervention Trial." *Journal of the American Medical Association* 258 (1987): 2388–95.

Medbo, J. I., A. C. Mohn, I. Tabata, R. Bahr, O. Vaage, and O. M. Sejersted. "Anaerobic Capacity Determined by Maximal Accumulated O_2 Deficit." *Journal of Applied Physiology* 64 (1988): 50–60.

Medbo, J. I., and I. Tabata. "Relative Importance of Aerobic and Anaerobic Energy Release During Shortlasting, Exhausting Bicycle Exercise." *Journal of Applied Physiology* 61 (1989): 1881–86.

National Heart, Lung and Blood Institute. *Exercise and Your Heart*. Washington, DC: U.S. Public Health Service, 1981.

Paffenbarger, R. S., and R. T. Hyde. "Exercise as Protection Against Heart Disease." *New England Journal of Medicine* 302 (1980): 1026.

Paffenbarger, R. S., and Wing, A. "Chronic Disease in Former College Students XI. Early Precursors of Non-Fatal Stroke." *American Journal of Epidemiology* 94, no. 6 (1971).

Paffenbarger, R. S., et al. "Chronic Disease in Former College Students II. Methods of Study and Observations of Mortality from Coronary Heart Disease." *American Journal of Public Health* 56, no. 6 (June 1966).

Paffenbarger, R. S., et al. "Physical Activity as an Index of Heart Attack Risk in College Alumni." *American Journal of Epidemiology* 108 (1978): 161–175.

Paffenbarger, R. S., R. T. Hyde, A. L. Wing, and C. Hsieh. "Physical Activity and All-Cause Mortality, and Longevity of College Alumni." *New England Journal of Medicine* 314 (1986): 605–13.

Paffenbarger, R. S., Jr., R. T. Hyde, A. L. Wing, I. M. Lee, D. L. Jung, and J. B. Kampert. "The Association of Changes in Physical-Activity Level and Other Lifestyle Characteristics with Mortality Among Men." *New England Journal of Medicine* 328 (1993): 538–545.

Peterson, G. E., and T. D. Fahey. "HDL-C in Five Elite Athletes Using Anabolic-Androgenic Steroids." *Physicians and Sportsmedicine* 12, no. 6 (1984): 120–130.

Pollock, M. L., et al. "Effects of Frequency and Duration of Training on Attrition and Incidence of Injury." *Medical Science* 9, no. 1 (1977): 31–6.

Saltin, B. "Anaerobic Capacity. Past, Present and Prospective." In: *Biochemistry of Exercise VII*, A. W. Taylor, P. D. Gollnick, H. J. Green, C. D. Ianuzzo, E. G. Noble, G. Metevier, and J. R. Sutton (eds.), 387-412. Champaign, IL: Human Kinetics Pub., 1990.

Saltin, B., G. Blomqvist, J. Mitchell, R. L. Johnson, K. Wildenthal, and C. B. Chapman. "Response to Exercise After Bed Rest and After Training." *Circulation* 37, 38, Suppl. 7 (1968): 1–78.

Sahlin, K. "Muscle Fatigue and Lactic Acid Accumulation." *Acta Physiologica Scandinavica* 128, Suppl. 556 (1986): 83–91.

Scheuer, J., and C. M. Tipton. "Cardiovascular Adaptations to Training." *Annual Review of Physiology* 39 (1977): 221.

Siscovick, D. S., N. S. Weiss, R. H. Fletcher, and T. Lasky. "The Incidence of Primary Cardiac Arrest During Vigorous Exercise." *New England Journal of Medicine* 311 (1984): 874–77.

Stone, W. J. "Exercise and Long-Term CV Risk Reduction in Corporate Executives." *Health Education* 14 (1983): 88.

Thorland, W. G., and T. B. Gilliam. "Comparison of Serum Lipids between Habitually High and Low Active Pre-Adolescent Males." *Medicine and Science in Sports and Exercise* 13 (1981): 316.

U. S. Center for Disease Control and Prevention and American College of Sports Medicine. *Workshop on Physical Activity and Public Health: Summary Statement*. Atlanta, Georgia, 1993.

U. S. Consensus Development Conference. "Lowering Blood Cholesterol to Prevent Heart Disease." *Journal of the American Medical Association* 253 (1986): 2080–86.

Van Camp, S. "Exercise-Related Sudden Death: Risks and Causes (part 1 of 2)." *Physicians and Sportsmedicine* 16, no. 5 (1988): 96–112.

Van Camp, S. "Exercise-Related Sudden Death: Cardiovascular Evaluation of Exercisers (part 2 of 2)." *Physicians and Sportsmedicine* 16, no. 6 (1988): 47–54.

Wallin, C. C., and J. S. Schendel. "Physiological Changes in Middle-Aged Men Following a Ten-Week Jogging Program." *Research Quarterly* 40, no. 3.

Watts, G. F., et al. "Effects on Coronary Artery Disease of Lipid-Lowering Diet, or Diet Plus Cholestyramine, in the St. Thomas' Atheosclerosis Regression Study (STARS)." *The Lancet* 339 (1992): 563-569.

Weinter, D. A., M. D. "Exercise Stress Testing." *New England Journal of Medicine* 30, no. 5 (August 1979): 230.

Wenger, H. A., and G. J. Bell. "The Interactions of Intensity, Frequency and Duration of Exercise Training in Altering Cardiorespiratory Fitness." *Sports Medicine* 3 (1986): 346–56.

White, J. R. "EKG Changes Using Carotid Artery for Heart Rate Monitoring." *Medical Science* 9, no. 2 (1977): 88–94.

Wilmore, J. H., et al. "Physiological Alterations Resulting from a 10-Week Program of Jogging." *Medical Science* 2, no. 1 (1970): 7–16.

Body Composition

The roles of both diet and exercise in achieving and maintaining a desirable body composition can be presented during a lecture-discussion session capitalizing on the transparencies and Fitness Profiles. Lab Worksheet 4-1 can be used either as a lead-in to the lesson or as a clinching tool afterward. We do recommend that the instructor review Chapter 9, Model Weight Management Program, before planning the Chapter 4 lesson.

OVERVIEW

OBJECTIVE	CONTENT SUMMARY	TRANSP.	LAB WKSHT.	PROFILE
Differentiate between overweight, overfat, and obesity.	The term *overweight* usually refers to status on the popular height-weight chart; it is not necessarily a reflection of body composition.	26	4-1	
	Overfat refers to a condition of 20% to 25% body fat in males and 30% to 35% in females.			
	Obesity refers to a condition of over 25% body fat in males and over 35% in females.			
	Excess body fat is related to the size and number of fat cells in the body. Fat people have more fat cells than thin people, and their cells are larger in size.			
	The number of fat cells probably remains constant from about adolescence onward.			

15

OBJECTIVE	CONTENT SUMMARY	TRANSP.	LAB WKSHT.	PROFILE
Recognize how calorie balance affects the gain or loss of body fat.	A calorie (kilocalorie) is the heat required to raise the temperature of one gram of water one degree centigrade. All energy used (exercise) and energy taken in (food) can be measured in calories. One pound of fat is equal to about 3,500 calories.	27	4-1	
	Neutral calorie balance: food intake equals energy output. Weight will not change. Positive calorie balance: food intake is greater than energy output. The extra calorie intake will be stored as fat. Negative calorie balance: energy output exceeds food intake. Body fat is usually reduced as it is burned for energy purposes.	27	4-1	
Identify the limitations of crash diets for reducing body fat.	Crash diets often require drastic, difficult-to-sustain changes in eating habits. Some crash diets overemphasize certain foods to the exclusion of others that may be nutritionally essential. An increase in physical activity requires a balanced diet. A crash diet occurring simultaneously may lead to health problems.	28		
Appreciate the relationship of exercise and diet to fat loss programs.	A combination of diet and exercise produces the most effective program for controlling body composition. A negative calorie balance of 1,000 calories per week could result in a loss of 15 pounds in one year. When a negative calorie balance is the result of diet alone, lean muscle tissue is lost along with fat.		4-1	

OBJECTIVE	CONTENT SUMMARY	TRANSP.	LAB WKSHT.	PROFILE
Recognize the elements of an effective exercise program for changing or controlling body composition.	A reasonable goal for weight loss is one pound per week.		4-1	
	CRE or aerobic activities represent the best exercise choices for controlling body fat.	29		4-1
	Duration and frequency of exercise are the most important ingredients of an exercise program designed to influence body composition.	30		
	For most people, a duration of thirty minutes and a frequency of three times per week seem to be minimum for altering body composition and achieving weight loss.		4-1	
	Active household and other routine chores can be helpful adjuncts to an exercise program geared for altering body composition.	31		4-2
	Sedentary activities do not burn enough calories to be useful in a fat reduction program.	32		4-3
Identify common myths connected to efforts to change body composition.	Except for exceedingly strenuous and prolonged activity, appetite does not tend to increase with regular exercise.		4-1	
	Exercise does not cause fat loss in specific body areas. Stored fat belongs to the whole body, not to the area in which it is stored. CRE exercises are best for losing body fat.			
	Wearing a rubber suit during exercise may lead to a large loss of body water but is not more effective in achieving fat loss.			
	Vibrators, massage, and saunas are useless for weight loss because they do not promote any significant burning of calories.			

Chapter Guides

OBJECTIVE	CONTENT SUMMARY	TRANSP.	LAB WKSHT.	PROFILE
	Weight training can be useful because it promotes muscle development and a favorable fat-muscle ratio.		4-1	
	Exercise can lead to weight gain if a negative calorie balance is avoided, and if the chosen activity promotes the development of muscle tissue.			
	Muscle tissue is lost gradually when a person becomes inactive. If food intake remains unchanged, a positive calorie balance will occur and the body will store the excessive intake as fat.			

References

American College of Sports Medicine. "Weight Loss in Wrestlers: Positon Stand of American College of Sports Medicine." In *P. E. Conditioning and Physical Fitness*, P. E. Allsen (ed.). Dubuque, IA: Wm. C. Brown Publishers, 1978.

American College of Sports Medicine. "Proper and Improper Weight Loss Programs." *Medical Science Sports Exercise* 15 (1983): ix–xiii.

Ashwell, M., and C. J. Meade. "Obesity: Can Some Fat Cells Enlarge While Others Are Shrinking?" *Lipids* 16 (1981): 475.

Ballor, D. L., V. L. Katch, M. D. Becque, et al. "Resistance Weight Training During Caloric Restriction Enhances Lean Body Weight Maintenance." *American Journal of Clinical Nutrition* 45, no. 1 (1988): 19–25.

Bennet, W., and J. Gurin. *The Dieter's Dilemma*. New York: Basic Books, 1982.

Clark, H. H. (ed.). "Exercise and Fat Reduction." *Physical Fitness Research Digest* 5 (1975): 1.

Cureton, K. J. "Effect of Experimental Alterations in Excess Weight on Aerobic Capacity and Distance Running Performance." *Medicine and Science in Sports* 10, no. 3 (February 1978): 194–99.

Dorghetti, P., K. Jensen, and T. S. Nelsen. "The Total Estimated Metabolic Cost of Rowing." *FISA Coach* 2(2): 1–4. 1991.

Faria, I. "Anthropometric and Physiologic Profile of a Cyclist - Age 70." *Medicine and Science in Sports* 9, no. 2 (January 1977): 118.

Gale, J. B. "Maximal Oxygen Consumption and Relative Body Fat of High-Ability Wrestlers." *Medicine and Science in Sports* 6, no. 4 (July 1974): 232-34.

Horton, E. "The Role of Exercise in the Treatment of Hypertension in Obesity." *International Journal of Obesity* 5, suppl. 1 (1981): 165-71.

Houston, M. E., D. A. Marrin, H. J. Green, and J. A. Thomson. "The Effect of Rapid Weight Loss on Physiological Functions in Wrestlers." *Physician and Sportsmedicine* 9 (1981): 73–78.

Katch, F. I., A. R. Behnke, and V. L. Katch. "Estimation of Body Fat from Skinfolds and Surface Area." *Human Biology* 51 (1980): 249.

Katch, F. I., and V. L. Katch. "Measurement and Prediction Errors in Body Composition Assessment and the Search for the Perfect Prediction Equation." *Research Quarterly of Exercise and Sport* 51 (1980): 249.

Katch, F. I., and W. D. McArdle. *Nutrition, Weight Control, and Exercise*. Philadelphia: Lea and Febiger, 1982.

Lamb, L. "Dangerous Dieting." *The Health Letter* 16, no. 2 (25 July 1980): 1–4.

Lamb, L. E. *The Weighting Game*. Secaucus, NJ: Lyle Stuart, Inc., 1988.

Lamb, L. E. "Sensible Weight Control." *The Health Letter* 40, no. 8 (August 1993): 144-1–144-10.

Leon, A. S., et al. "Effects of a Vigorous Walking Program on Body Composition, and Carbohydrate and Lipid Metabolism of Obese Young Men." *American Journal of Clinical Nutrition* 32 (1979): 1976.

Lohman, T. G. "Skinfold and Body Density and Their Relation to Body Fatness: A Review." *Human Biology* 53 (1981): 181.

Mann, G. V. "The Influence of Obesity on Health." *The New England Journal of Medicine* (1 August 1974): 226–232.

Newsholme, E. A. "Sounding Board: A Possible Metabolic Basis for the Control of Body Weight." *The New England Journal of Medicine* 302, no. 7 (14 February 1980): 400.

Oscai, L. B. "Exercise of Food Restriction: Effect on Adipose Tissue Cellularity." *American Journal of Physiology* 227, no. 4 (1974): 902.

Pavlou, K. N., W. P. Steffee, R. H. Learman, and B. A. Burrows. "Effects of Dieting and Exercise on Lean Body Mass, Oxygen Uptake, and Strength." *Medical Science Sports Exercises* 17 (1985): 466–71.

Pollock, M., et al. "Effects of Walking on Body Composition and Cardiovascular Function of Middle-Aged Men." *Journal of Applied Physiology* 30, no. 1 (January 1971): 126-9.

Schwartz, B. *Diets Don't Work*. Houston, TX: Breakthru Pub., 1982.

Sours, H. E., et al. "Sudden Death Associated with Very Low Calorie Weight Reduction Regimens." *American Journal of Clinical Nutrition* 35 (1981): 453.

Tufts University Diet and Nutrition Letter. "First, Understand What Causes Weight Gain." *Tufts University Diet and Nutrition Letter* 3, no. 11 (January 1986): 3–6.

United States Department of Agriculture. *Food and Your Weight* (HG74). Washington, DC: Superintendent of Documents, 1977.

University of California, Berkeley, Wellness Letter. "Wrap-up: Weight, Overweight, Obesity." *University of California, Berkeley, Wellness Letter* 2, no. 8 (May 1986): 4.

Wilmore, J. H. "Body Composition and Strength Development." *Journal of Physical Education and Recreation* 46, no. 1 (January 1975): 38.

Wilmore, J. H. "Alterations in Strength, Body Composition, and Anthropometric Measurements Consequent to a 10-Week Weight Training Program." *Medicine and Science in Sports* 6 (1974): 133.

Wilmore, J. H., et al. "Body Composition Changes with a 10-Week Program of Jogging." *Medical Science* 2, no. 3 (Fall 1970): 113–17.

Work, J. A. "Exercise for the Overweight Patient." *Physician and Sportsmedicine* 18, no. 7 (July 1990): 113–122.

Zuti, W. B., and L. A. Golding. "Comparing Diet and Exercise as Weight Reduction Tools." *Physician and Sportsmedicine* 4 (1976): 49.

Muscular Strength, Muscular Endurance, and Flexibility

The information necessary for designing an exercise program aimed at developing the qualities of muscular fitness — muscular strength, muscular endurance, and flexibility— can be presented during lecture-discussion. The appropriate transparencies provide a flexible lecture framework at the instructor's discretion. Worksheet 5-1 can be used to prepare students for the lecture-discussion, or it can be assigned afterward as a clinching tool.

OVERVIEW

OBJECTIVE	CONTENT SUMMARY	TRANSP.	LAB WKSHT.	PROFILE
Differentiate between muscular strength and muscular endurance.	*Muscular strength* is the ability to exert maximum force, usually in a single exertion.	33 34	5-1	
	Muscular endurance is the ability to repeat a muscle contraction against resistance over and over again or to hold a muscle in a contracted position for an extended period of time.	33		

OBJECTIVE	CONTENT SUMMARY	TRANSP.	LAB WKSHT.	PROFILE
Recognize how muscles and nerves work together.	The nervous system orchestrates the action of muscles, tendons, and bones. Muscles are composed of numerous individual muscle fibers, which are stored in motor units. The number of units and fibers that are called on to act will vary, depending on the force that is needed; however, those fibers that do contract do so maximally.		5-1	
Recognize how muscle use and disuse influence atrophy and hypertrophy.	The number of fibers and units do not seem to change during the lifetime; however, the size of the fiber can change. An increase in size is *hypertrophy*. Decrease in size is *atrophy*. There is a direct relationship between size and strength.	35	5-1	
Differentiate among isotonic, isometric, and isokinetic muscle contractions.	There are three types of muscle contractions. *Isotonic* contractions produce strength through a full range of motion against a fixed resistance. *Isometric* contractions produce strength without movement, and only at the point of contraction. *Isokinetic* contractions are similar to isotonic except that the resistance is variable to conform to the different levels of strength that exist throughout the range of motion.	36		

OBJECTIVE	CONTENT SUMMARY	TRANSP.	LAB WKSHT.	PROFILE
Identify how weight training develops strength and endurance.	Weight training is isotonic exercise that uses free weights or machines that provide resistance.	37	5-1	
	By adjusting the amount of weight lifted and the repetitions, weight training can be adapted to emphasize either muscular strength or muscular endurance. Heavy resistance with few repetitions works best for development of muscular strength. Light resistance with many repetitions is the key to muscular endurance.			
Differentiate between weight training and weight lifting.	Weight lifting is a competitive sport in which the person who lifts the most weight wins.			
	Weight training is not competitive except for body builders.			
Recognize various myths connected to weight training.	Weight training is useful for building strength and endurance in women without causing overmuscularization.	38	5-1	
	Weight training can increase the ratio of muscle to fat.			
	It is safe to begin weight training in early adolescence.			
	People of all ages can benefit from a sound weight training program.			
	Weight training can influence the appearance of the bust by strengthening the pectoral muscles.			
	Calisthenics do less for muscular strength than they do for endurance, when compared with weight training.			

OBJECTIVE	CONTENT SUMMARY	TRANSP.	LAB WKSHT.	PROFILE
Recognize problems connected to strength and endurance development.	Some exercises should be avoided. Exercise-induced muscle soreness may be limited by avoiding negative work. Muscular fitness may be pursued even with orthopedic problems.	39		
Recognize how flexibility serves to prevent muscle and joint problems.	Flexibility is the ability to flex and extend a joint through a normal range of movement. Joints that are regularly moved through their full range of motion, and muscles that regularly flex and extend fully, retain full mobility. Good flexibility enhances sports performance and helps to avoid injuries connected to rapid and vigorous movement.	40 41	5-1	5–1
Differentiate between the advantages of ballistic and static stretching.	Ballistic stretching is characterized by bouncing or bobbing movements. This approach may cause the stretching muscles to contract defensively. Static stretching represents a gradual stretching that offers less risk of injury due to overstretching as well as less risk of muscle soreness.		5-1	

References

American Academy of Pediatrics. "Weight Training and Weight Lifting: Information for the Pediatrician." *Physician and Sportsmedicine* 11 (1983): 157.

Anderson, T., and J. T. Kearney. "Effects of Three Resistance Training Programs on Muscular Strength and Absolute and Relative Endurance." *Research Quarterly for Exercise and Sport* 53 (1982): 1.

Arendt, E. A. "Strength Development: A Comparison of Resistive Exercise Techniques." *Contemporary Orthopedics* 9 (1984): 1–73.

Armstrong, R. B. "Mechanisms of Exercise-Induced Delayed Onset Muscular Soreness: A Brief Review." *Medicine and Science in Sports Exercise* 6 (1984): 529-38.

Atha, J. "Strengthening Muscle." *Exercise and Sport Sciences Reviews* 9 (1981): 1–73.

Beaulieu, J. "Developing a Stretching Program." *Physician and Sportsmedicine* 9 (November 1981): 59–69.

Braith, R. W., J. E. Graves, M. L. Pollock, S. L. Leggett, D. M. Carpenter, and A. B. Colvin. "Comparison of Two versus Three Days per Week of Variable Resistance Training During 10 and 18 Week Programs." *International Journal of Sports Medicine* 10 (1989): 450–54.

Fahey, T. D. *Basic Weight Training.* Mountain View, CA: Mayfield Publishing Co., 1989.

Fardy, P. S. "Isometric Exercise and the Cardiovascular System." *Physician and Sportsmedicine* 9 (September 1981): 44.

Fitzgerald, B., and G. McLatchie. "Degenerative Joint Disease in Weightlifters. Fact or Fiction." *British Journal of Sports Medicine* 14 (1980): 97–101.

Fleck, S. J. "Cardiovascular Response to Strength Training." In: *Strength and Power in Sport.* P. C. Komi (ed.). (Oxford, Blackwell Scientific, 1992): 305–315.

Fleck, S. J., and W. J. Kraemer. "Resistance-Training: Physiological Responses and Adaptations." *Physician and Sportsmedicine* 16 (1988): 108–24.

Garnica, R. A. "Muscular Power in Young Women After Slow and Fast Isokinetic Training." *Journal of Orthopedic Sports Physical Therapy.* 8 (1986): 255-63.

Gettman, L. R. "The Effect of Circuit Weight Training on Strength, Cardiorespiratory Function, and Body Composition of Adult Men. *Medicine and Science in Sports and Exercise* 10, no. 3 (February 1978): 171–6.

Gharote, M. L. "Effect of Yoga Exercises on Failures on the Kraus-Weber Tests." *Perceptual and Motor Skills* 43 (1976): 654.

Gillam, G. M. "Effects of Frequency of Weight Training on Muscle Strength Enhancement." *Journal of Sports Medicine* 21 (1981): 432-36.

Graves, J. E., M. L. Pollock, S. H. Leggett, R. Braith, D. M. Carpenter, and L. E. Bishop. "Effect of Reduced Training Frequency on Muscular Strength." *Internatonal Journal of Sports Medicine* 9 (1988): 316–19.

Graves, J. E., M. L. Pollock, A. E. Jones, A. B. Colvin, and S. H. Legett. "Specificity of Limited Range of Motion Variable Resistance Training," *Medicine and Science in Sports and Exercise* 21 (1989): 84–89.

Hatfield, F. C. *Bodybuilding: A Scientific Approach.* Chicago: Contemporary Books, 1984.

Hedrick, A. "Flexibility and the Conditioning Program." *National Strength Conditioning Association Journal* 15, no. 4 (1993): 62–66.

Hickson, R. C. "Interference of Strength Development by Simultaneously Training for Strength and Endurance." *European Journal of Applied Physiology* 45 (1980): 255–63.

Jackson, A., T. Jackson, J. Hnatak, and J. West."Strength Development: Using Functional Isometrics in an Isotonic Strength Training Program."*Research Quarterly of Exercise and Sport* 56 (1985): 234-47.

Katch, V., et al. "Muscular Development and Lean Body Weight in Body Builders and Weight Lifters." *Medicine and Science in Sports and Exercise* 12 (1980): 340.

MacDougall, J. D., D. Tuxen, D. G. Sale, J. R. Moroz, and J. R. Sutton. "Arterial Blood Pressure Response to Heavy Resistance Training." *Journal of Applied Physiology* 58 (1985): 785–90.

MacDougall, J. D., D. G. Sale, S. E. Alway, and J. R. Sutton. "Muscle Fiber Number in Biceps Brachii in Body Builders and Control Subjects." *Journal of Applied Physiology* 57 (1984): 1399–1403.

MacDougall, J. D., et al. "Muscle Ultrastructural Characteristics of Elite Powerlifters and Bodybuilders." *European Journal of Applied Physiology* 48 (1982): 117.

MacDougall, J. D., G. R. Ward, D. G. Sale, and J. R. Sutton. "Biochemical Adaptation of Human Skeletal Muscle to Heavy Resistance Training and Immobilization." *Journal of Applied Physiology* 43 (1977): 700–703.

Marcinik, E. J., J. Potts, G. Schlabach, S. Will, P. Dawson, and B. F. Hurley. "Effects of Strength Training on Lactate Threshold and Endurance Performance." *Medicine and Science in Sports and Exercise* 23 (1991): 739–743..

McCully, K. K., and J. A. Faulkner. "Characteristics of Lengthening Contractions Associated with Injury to Skeletal Muscle Fibers." *Journal of Applied Physiology* 61 (1986): 293–99.

McGee, D. S., T. C. Jesse, M. H. Stone, and D. Blessing. "Leg and Hip Endurance Adaptations to Three Different Weight-Training Programs." *Journal of Applied Sport Science Research* 6, no. 2 (1992): 92–95.

Millar, A. P. "An Early Stretching Routine for Calf Muscle Strains." *Medical Science* 8 (1976): 39–42.

O'Bryant, H. S., R. Byrd, and M. H. Stone. "Cycle Ergometer Performance and Maximum Leg and Hip Strength Adaptations to Two Different Methods of Weight-Training." *Journal of Applied Sport Science Research* 2 (1988): 27–30.

Pearl, B., and Moran, G. T. *Getting Stronger.* Bolinas, CA: Shelter Publications, 1986.

Rasch, P. J., and F. L. Allman, Jr. "Controversial Exercises." *Journal of American Corrective Therapy* 26, no. 4 (July-August 1972): 95.

Sale, D. G. "Neural Adaptation to Resistance Training." *Medicine and Science in Sports and Exercise* 20, suppl. (1988): 135–45.

Schulz, P. "Flexibility: Day of the Static Stretch." *Physician and Sportsmedicine* 7 (1979): 109.

Stauber, W. T. "Eccentric Action of Muscles: Physiology, Injuries and Adaptation." *Exercise and Sports Science Reviews* 17 (1989): 157–85.

Stone, M. "Muscle Conditioning and Muscle Injuries." *Medicine and Science in Sports and Exercise* 22, no. 4 (August 1990): 457–462.

Stone, M. H. "Implications for Connective Tissue and Bone Alterations Resulting from Resistance Exercise Training." *Medicine and Science in Sports and Exercise* 20, Suppl. (1988): 162–68.

Stone, M. H., S. J. Fleck, N. T. Triplett, and W. J. Kraemer. "Health and Performance Related Potential of Resistance Training." *Sports Medicine* 11 (1991): 210–231.

Thorstensson, A., et al. "Muscular Strength and Fiber Composition in Athletes and Sedentary Men." *Medical Science* 9, no. 1 (1977): 26–30.

Wilmore, J. H. "Alterations in Strength, Body Composition, and Anthropometric Measurements Consequent to a 10-Week Weight Training Program." *Medicine and Science in Sports* 6 (1974): 133.

Wilmore, J. H. "Physiological Alterations Consequent to Circuit Weight Training." *Medicine and Science in Sports and Exercise* 10, no. 2 (1978): 79–84.

6 Model Exercise Programs and Appendix B

Chapter 6 and Appendix B contain all of the information necessary for the student to select activities and exercise systems to design a personal program. Appendix B contains detailed information about sports and activities as well as the models presented in Chapter 6. Although the instructor can introduce the various model programs during a lecture, it may be more effective to do so during laboratory (activity) sessions. The transparencies for Chapter 6 have been prepared so that the instructor can underscore and clarify each of the different model programs. The Appendix B transparency presents some examples of sports and activities so that the instructor can clarify the meaning of the activity ratings. Worksheet 6-1 provides an opportunity for the student to record the results of having tried the various models as well as other activities of choice.

OVERVIEW

OBJECTIVE	CONTENT SUMMARY	TRANSP.	LAB WKSHT.	PROFILE
Differentiate from among model programs.	The selection of a particular fitness program should be based on its potential to achieve specific fitness goals.	42	6-1	
	Walking, jogging, and running are activities that, when sustained, burn large numbers of calories and therefore are excellent activities for achieving CRE and body composition goals.	43		
	Choosing a particular walking, jogging, or running program should be based on one's CRE fitness level.	44		

OBJECTIVE	CONTENT SUMMARY	TRANSP.	LAB WKSHT.	PROFILE
	An evenly paced, sustained approach to walking or jogging is an effective way to achieve benefits.			
	Interval training can effectively combine walking and jogging.	45		
	Racing requires careful preparation and clear goals.			
	Interval circuit training using combinations of exercise equipment can effectively develop all five fitness components.	46 to 49		
	Calisthenics circuit training combines a series of exercises and time goals into an effective program.	50 to 52		
	Calisthenics can be used for effective stretching and warm-up prior to other physical activity.	53 to 55		
	Swimming, bicycling, and rope skipping are popular and effective activities for achieving CRE and body composition goals.	56 57		
	Weight training is one of the most effective ways to develop both muscular strength and muscular endurance.	58 59		
Select and pursue one or more model programs consistent with your personal goals.	The student should be assigned to try out several or more of the model programs. Transparencies 42–60 can help the instructor clarify all of the models desired. Lab Worksheet 6-1 and other progress cards can be used so that the student can become familiar with exercise record-keeping.		6-1	
Identify potential benefits of varied sports and activities.	A wide variety of sports and activities are available to choose from in order to achieve specific fitness goals.	60		

Chapter Guides

OBJECTIVE	CONTENT SUMMARY	TRANSP.	LAB WKSHT.	PROFILE
Select activities consistent with specific fitness goals.	The student can try activities that are appealing and consistent with personal fitness goals. These can be noted on Lab Worksheet 6-1. Activities can be selected from Appendix B as well as from Chapter 6.		6-1	

References

American Heart Association. *Jump for the Health of It.* Dallas, TX: American Heart Association, 1983.

Beaulieu, J. E. "Developing a Stretching Program." *Physician and Sportsmedicine* 9 (1981): 59.

Chandler, T. J., G. D. Wilson, and M. H. Stone. "The Effect of the Squat Exercise on Knee Stability." *Medicine and Science in Sports and Exercise* 21 (1989): 299–303.

Clarke, H. "Jogging." *Physical Fitness Research Digest* 7 (January 1977): 1–23.

Clarke, H. "Swimming and Bicycling." *Physical Fitness Research Digest* 7 (July 1977): 1–22.

Daniels, J. T. "A Physiologist's View of Running Economy." *Medicine and Science in Sports and Exercise* 17 (1985): 322–38.

Fellingham, G. W. "Caloric Cost of Walking and Running." *Medicine and Science in Sports* 10, no. 2 (1978): 132–36.

Fleck, S. J., and W. J. Kraemer. *Designing Resistance Training Programs.* Champaign, IL: Human Kinetics Books, 1987.

Fox, E., D. Matthews, and J. Bairstow. *Interval Training for Lifetime Fitness.* New York: Dial Press, 1980.

Gossard, D., W. L. Haskell, B. Taylor, et al. "Effects of Low- and High-Intensity Home-Based Exercise Training on Functional Capacity in Healthy Middle-Age Men." *American Journal of Cardiology* 57 (1986): 446–49.

Getchell, B., and P. Cleary. "The Caloric Costs of Rope Skipping and Running." *Physician and Sportsmedicine* 8 (1980): 56.

Hakkinen, K. "Factors Influencing Trainability of Muscular Strength During Short Term and Prolonged Training." *National Strength and Conditioning Association Journal* 7 (1985): 32–34.

Howley, E. T. "The Caloric Costs of Running and Walking One Mile for Men and Women." *Medicine and Science in Sports* 6, no. 4 (April 1974): 235–37.

Hurley, B. F., D. R. Seals, A. A. Ehsani, et al. "Effects of High-Intensity Strength Training on Cardiovascular Function. *Medicine and Science in Sports and Exercise* 16 (1984): 483–88.

Jette, M., J. Mongeon, and R. Routhier. "The Energy Cost of Rope Skipping." *Journal of Sports Medicine* 19 (1979).

Martin, B. J. "The Effect of Warm-Up on Metabolic Responses to Strenuous Exercise." *Medical Science* 7, no. 2 (1975): 146–49.

Martin, W. H., J. Montgomery, P. G. Snell, et al. "Cardiovascular Adaptations to Intense Swim Training in Sedentary Middle-Aged Men and Women." *Circulation* 75 (1987): 323–30.

Messier, J. P., and M. Dill. "Alterations in Strength and Maximal Oxygen Uptake Consequent to Nautilus Circuit Weight Training. *Research Quarterly of Exercise and Sport* 56 (1985): 345–51.

Nosse, L. J., and G. R. Hunter. "Free Weights: A Review Supporting Their Use in Training and Rehabilitation." *Athletic Training* 20 (1985): 206–209.

O'Brien. "Aerobic/Calisthenic and Aerobic/Circuit Weight Training Programs for Navy Men: A Comparative Study." *Medicine and Science in Sports and Exercise* 17 (1985): 482–87.

O'Shea, J. P., C. Novak, and F. Gaulard. "Bicycle Interval Training for Cardiovascular Fitness." *Physician and Sportsmedicine* 10 (1982): 156.

Rasch, P. J. *Weight Training.* 4th ed. Dubuque, IA: Wm. C. Brown Publishers, 1982.

Santiago, M. C., J. F. Alexander, G. A. Stull, R. C. Serfrass, A. M. Hayday, and A. S. Leon. "Physiological Responses of Sedentary Women to a 20-Week Continuing Program of Walking or Jogging." *Scandinavian Journal of Sports Science* 9 (1987): 33–39.

Schultz, P. "Flexibility: Day of the Static Stretch." *Physician and Sportsmedicine* 7 (November 1979): 109.

Schultz, P. "Walking for Fitness: Slow but Sure." *Physician and Sportsmedicine* 8 (1980): 24.

Sharp, R. L., D. L. Costill, W. J. Fink, and D. S. King. "Effects of Eight Weeks of Bicycle Ergometer Sprint Training on Buffer Capacity. *International Journal of Sports Medicine* 7 (1983): 13-17.

Town, G. P., et al. "The Effect of Rope Skipping Rate on Energy Expenditure of Males and Females." *Medicine and Science in Sports and Exercise* 12 (1980): 295.

Webb, P., W. H. M. Saris, P. F. M. Schoffelen, G. J. van Ingen Schenau, and F. ten Hoor. "Work in Walking." *Medicine and Science in Sports and Exercise* 20 (1988): 331–37.

Wilmore, J., et al. "Energy Cost of Circuit Weight Training." *Medicine and Science in Sports* 10 (1978): 79.

Appendix B

De Meersman, R. E. "Effects of Judo Instruction on Cardiorespiratory Parameters." *Journal of Sports Medicine* 17 (1977): 169.

Ellfeldt, L. "Aerobic Dance (Not Really Dance At All)." *Journal of Physical Education and Recreation* 48, no. 5 (May 1977): 45.

Getchell, L. H. "Energy Cost of Playing Golf." *Arch, Phys. Med. & Rehab.* 49, no. 1 (1968): 31.

Lyons, J. W., and R. E. Porter. "Cross-Country Skiing." *Journal of the American Medical Association* 239, no. 4 (23 January 1978): 334-35.

Richie, D. H., S. F. Kelso, and P. A. Bellucci. "Aerobic Dance Injuries: A Retrospective Study of Instructors and Participants." *Physician and Sportsmedicine* 13 (1985): 130-140.

Smodlaka, V. N. "Cardiovascular Aspects of Soccer." *Physician and Sportsmedicine* 6, no. 7 (July 1978).

7 Getting Started and Keeping Going

A lecture-discussion format can utilize the transparencies and the fitness profiles to orient students to the five steps of the start-up and program maintenance process. Otherwise the elements of the chapter are designed as laboratory experiences. Additional lecture-discussion sessions can follow up on student experiences with suggestions offered to assist progress with program plans. Individual conferences with students can be helpful in monitoring their progress as well as recommending program plan adjustments where they may be needed.

OVERVIEW

OBJECTIVE	CONTENT SUMMARY	TRANSP.	LAB WKSHT.	PROFILE
List goals.	Clear goals provide direction to a fitness program.	61		7-1
Select activities.	Activities should be selected based on criteria that can help assure success.	62		
Design a weekly program plan.	A fitness plan should contain specific activities along with progressive overload information.	61 64		7-1
Sign a contractual commitment.	A written contract can help solidify one's commitment to an exercise program.	61	7-1	7-1

OBJECTIVE	CONTENT SUMMARY	TRANSP.	LAB WKSHT.	PROFILE
Identify steps to maximize program compliance.	Program compliance can be maximized by recognizing certain compliance tips.	63	7-1	
Appreciate the value of recording program progress.	Keeping a record of progress can help to provide a sense of accomplishment as well as a commitment reminder.	65	7-1	

References

Pollock, M. L. "Prescribing Exercise for Fitness and Adherence." In: *Exercise Adherence: Its Impact on Public Health*, R. K. Dishman (ed.), 259–277. Champaign, IL: Human Kinetics Books, 1988.

Rejeski, W. J., and E. A. Kenney, *Fitness Motivation*. Champaign, IL: Human Kinetics Books, 1988.

Sallis, J. F., and M. F. Hovell. "Determinants of Exercise Behavior." *Exercise and Sports Science Reviews* 18 (1990): 307–30.

Smith, T. "You're a Breed Apart! What Motivates You to Work Out?" *Running and Fitness Newsletter* 8, no. 10 (October 1990): 3.

8 Eating Right

This chapter provides basic information to help students make informed decisions about foods essential to good health and fitness. Chapter 4, "Body Composition," contains a foundation for those altering their muscle-to-fat ratio, while this chapter provides the nutrition side of the picture. A lecture-discussion format using the available transparencies can help reinforce student worksheet activities.

OVERVIEW

OBJECTIVE	CONTENT SUMMARY	TRANSP.	LAB WKSHT.	PROFILE
Identify essential nutrients.	Six categories of essential nutrients—proteins, carbohydrates, fats, minerals, and water—fulfill three primary functions in the body: • providing energy • building and repairing body tissue • regulating body processes	66	8-1	
Decide whether you need to change eating patterns.	U.S. Dietary Goals are aimed at reducing consumption of fats, refined sugar, cholesterol, and salt and at increasing the consumption of naturally occurring carbohydrates.	67 68	8-1	
Plan nutritionally balanced menus.	The Daily Food Guide groups are categories of foods that resemble each other nutritionally.	69	8-1	

OBJECTIVE	CONTENT SUMMARY	TRANSP.	LAB WKSHT.	PROFILE
Recognize why it is prudent to limit intake of salt, sugar, caffeine, saturated fat, and cholesterol.	High levels of blood cholesterol-containing, low-density lipoprotein have been implicated as a primary factor in heart disease.		8-1	
	Cholesterol intake should be limited to 300 mg. per day.	70		
	Saturated fat should be eliminated from the diet as much as possible.	71–72		
	Salt should be limited because its use is related to high blood pressure.			
	Refined sugar as used in soft drinks, candy, and sweet desserts provides "empty calories." Such sweets often replace foods with greater nutritional content and can lead to tooth decay and obesity.			
	Caffeine is a stimulant that has negative side effects.			
Assess need for food supplements.	Food supplements are generally necessary only when nutritional deficiencies exist. A balanced diet containing adequate helpings of foods from the Daily Food Guide is generally adequate for even the most vigorous exerciser.			
	Fiber intake can be beneficial, but its addition to the diet should be gradual.			
	Foods containing tropical oils should be avoided, because these oils are high in saturated fats.			
	Some athletes erroneously believe that protein, mineral, and vitamin supplements will improve performance.			

Chapter Guides

OBJECTIVE	CONTENT SUMMARY	TRANSP.	LAB WKSHT.	PROFILE
Recognize common misconceptions related to eating and exercise.	While caffeine may delay the onset of exhaustion during extended activity, it may also dangerously disguise the sensation of fatigue.		8-1	
	Easily digested foods, eaten about three hours before vigorous physical activity, is the recommended guideline.			
	Starvation regimens and "drying out" to meet weight classifications contain health risks.			
	Alcohol intake is contraindicated before exercise.			

References

Belko, A. Z. "Vitamins and Exercise—An Update." *Medicine and Science in Sports Exercise* 19, suppl. (1987): 191–96.

Bentivegna, A., et al. "Diet, Fitness and Athletic Performance." *Physician and Sports Medicine* 7 (1979): 99.

Blom, P. C. S., A. T. Hostmark, O. Vaage, K. R. Dardel, and S. Maehlum. "Effect of Different Post-Exercise Sugar Diets on the Rate of Muscle Glycogen Synthesis." *Medicine and Science in Sports and Exercise* 19 (1987): 491–96.

Bogert, L. J., et al. *Nutrition and Physical Fitness.* Philadelphia: W. B. Saunders Company, 1979.

Brooks, G. A. "Amino Acid and Protein Metabolism During Exercise and Recovery." *Medicine and Science in Sports and Exercise* 19, suppl. (1987): 150–56.

Butterfield, G., and D. Calloway. "Physical Activity Improves Protein Utilization in Young Men." *British Journal of Nutrition* 51 (1984): 171–84.

Food and Nutrition Board. National Research Council. *Recommended Dietary Allowances.* Washington, DC: National Academy of Sciences, 1980.

Gershoff, S., et al. *The Tufts University Guide to Total Nutrition.* New York: Harper & Row, 1990.

Goodhart, R. S., and M. E. Shils (eds.). *Modern Nutrition in Health and Disease,* 6th ed. Philadelphia: Lea & Febiger, 1980.

Haskell, W., J. Scala, and J. Whittam (eds.). *Nutrition and Athletic Performance.* Palo Alto, CA: Bull Publishing Co., 1982.

Haymes, E. M. "Nutritional Concerns: Needs for Iron." *Medicine and Science in Sports and Exercise* 19, suppl. (1987): 197–200.

Haymes, E. M. "The Use of Vitamin and Mineral Supplements by Athletes." *Journal of Drug Issues, Inc.* (Summer 1980): 361–69.

Herbert, V., and S. Barrett. *Vitamins and Health Food Robbers: The Great American Hustle.* Philadelphia: George F. Stickley Company, 1981.

Human Nutrition Information Service. "The Food Guide Pyramid." *United States Department of Agriculture* 252 (August 1992).

Lamb, L. E. "The Balanced Diet." *The Health Letter* special report 15 (1984): 1–4.

Lamb, L. E. "What to Eat for Exercise." *The Health Letter* 35, no. 11 (June 1990): 2–4.

Lamb, L. E. "Which Fat is Better?" *The Health Letter* 36, no. 7 (Oct. 1990): 3–5.

Liebman, B. "The HDL/Triglycerides Trap." *Nutrition Action Health Letter* 17, no. 7 (Sept. 1990): 1, 5–7.

Liebman, B. "The Changing American Diet." *Nutrition Action Health Letter* 17, no. 4 (May 1990): 8–9.

Parizkova, J., and V. A. Rogozkin. *Nutrition, Physical Fitness and Health.* Baltimore: University Park Press, 1978.

Pritikin, N. *Diet for Runners.* New York: Simon and Schuster, 1986.

Stamler, J. "Cutting Cholesterol." *Nutrition Action Health Letter* 16, no. 7 (Sept. 1989): 5–7.

Stamler, J. "Diet and Coronary Heart Disease." *Biometrics* 38 (1982): 95.

Tufts University Diet and Nutrition Letter. "Benefits of Eating Fish." *Tufts University Diet and Nutrition Letter* 3, no. 5 (July 1985): 1–3.

United States Department of Agriculture and United States Department of Health and Human Services. "Dietary Guidelines for Americans." *U. S. Government Printing Office* 3 (1990).

University of California, Berkeley, Wellness Letter. "Wrap-Up: Fiber." *University of California, Berkeley, Wellness Letter* 1, no. 11 (August 1985): 4–5.

University of California, Berkeley, Wellness Letter. "Wrap-Up: Vitamin Supplements." *University of California, Berkeley, Wellness Letter* 2, no. 1 (October 1985): 4–5.

University of California, Berkeley, Wellness Letter. "Fats: What You Need to Know." *University of California, Berkeley, Wellness Letter* 3, no. 1 (October 1986): 4–5.

University of California, Berkeley, Wellness Letter. "Our Vitamin Prescription: The Big Four." *University of California, Berkeley, Wellness Letter* 10, no. 4 (January 1994): 1–5.

Williams, M. H. *Nutrition for Fitness and Sport.* Dubuque, IA: Wm. C. Brown Publishers, 1983.

Williams, M. H. *Nutritional Aspects of Human Physical and Athletic Performance.* Springfield, IL: Charles C. Thomas, 1988.

Model Weight Management Program

The model weight loss program is an option for students whose goal is to reduce body fat. The instructor can help such students with the seven steps of the program by forming a special interest group (e.g.: "Fat Fighters," etc.) which could meet for 15 or 20 minutes during lab sessions. A trained fitness counselor or graduate student might be assigned to lead the group and to hold individual conferences with the students.

The transparencies related to the seven steps can be used to guide the special interest group. Completing Fitness Profiles 9-1A through 9-7 will carry the students through the entire process. Worksheet 9-1 is designed to help each student assess progress and problems.

OVERVIEW

OBJECTIVE	CONTENT SUMMARY	TRANSP.	LAB WKSHT.	PROFILE
List reasons for wanting to slim down.	Unless a person has important reasons for wanting to lose weight (fat), the effort will probably fail.	73		
Assess your daily calorie balance.	Use body fat assessment to calculate target weight and negative calorie goals. Or use the alternate method if body fat has not been assessed.	74 75	9-1	9-1A 9-1B
	Now calculate your current calorie balance by charting the amount of food you eat and how many calories you burn during activity. Do this for a week.	76 to 78		9-2 9-3 9-4

OBJECTIVE	CONTENT SUMMARY	TRANSP.	LAB WKSHT.	PROFILE
Develop a personal contract.	Complete a weight control contract by building on reasons for wanting to slim down. Include your estimated target weight. Your contract should describe your physical activity plan and the number of calories in your diet plan.	79	9-1	9-5
Plan well-balanced meals that meet your calorie intake goals.	Once your daily calorie intake goal is clear, plan daily menus for meals and snacks. It is best to plan for one week at a time.	80 to 82	9-1	9-6
Plan exercise to achieve calorie output goals.	You should seek daily routines that burn calories in addition to those calories burned through planned exercise. Quantify your exercise by referring to your personal contract.	83 79	9-1	9-5
Record program progress.	Weigh yourself at the same time each week and record your weight on the "Weight Control Progress Graph."	84		9-7
Identify steps to maximize compliance.	Tips for managing eating problems include: • eat planned meals and snacks • choose the right foods • limit amounts of food • change cues that trigger eating • avoid using foods to replace feelings • avoid storing troublesome foods • make wise choices when eating out	85 86	9-1	

Chapter Guides

References

American College of Sports Medicine. "Proper and Improper Weight Loss Programs." *Medicine and Science in Sports and Exercise* 15 (1983): ix-xiii.

American Dietetic Association. *Exchange Lists for Meal Planning*. Chicago: American Dietetic Association and American Diabetes Association, 1976.

Ballor, D. L., V. L. Katch, M. D. Becque, et al. "Resistance Weight Training During Caloric Restriction Enhances Lean Body Weight Maintenance." *American Journal of Clinical Nutrition* 47, no. 47 (1988): 19-25.

Consumer Reports Health Letter. "How to Lose Weight and Keep It Off." *Consumers Union* 2, no. 2 (February 1990): 9-11.

Ferguson, J. *Habits, Not Diets.* Palo Alto, CA: Bull Publishing, 1976.

Houston, M. E., D. A. Marrin, H. J. Green, and J. A. Thomson. "The Effect of Rapid Weight Loss on Physiological Functions in Wrestlers." *Physician and Sportsmedicine* 9 (1981): 73–78.

Lamb, L. E. "Exercise to Control Body Fat." *The Health Letter*, special report, 74 (1986): 1–4.

Leon, G. R. "The Behavior Modification Approach to Weight Reduction." *Contemporary Nutrition* 4 (1979).

Pavlou, K. N., W. P. Steffee, R. H. Learman, and B. A. Burrows. "Effects of Dieting and Exercise on Lean Body Mass, Oxygen Uptake, and Strength." *Medicine and Science in Sports and Exercise* 17 (1985): 466–71.

Stunkard, A. J., and S. B. Penick. "Behavior Modification in the Treatment of Obesity: The Problem of Maintaining Weight Loss." *Archives of General Psychiatry* 36 (1979): 801.

Tufts University Diet and Nutrition Newsletter. "Losing Weight and Making Sure You Keep It Off." *Tufts University Diet and Nutrition Newsletter* 3, no. 12 (February 1986): 3–5.

Zuti, W. B., and L. A. Golding. "Comparing Diet and Exercise as Weight Reduction Tools." *Physician and Sportsmedicine* 4 (1975): 49–53.

10 Managing Stress

This chapter contains a brief introduction to the subject of stress. The basic content of the chapter can be developed during a lecture-discussion session. If desired, one or more of the relaxation techniques can be tried out in class. The transparencies will support a lecture, while Lab Worksheet 10-1 can be used to reinforce the reading and the in-class sessions.

OVERVIEW

OBJECTIVE	CONTENT SUMMARY	TRANSP.	LAB WKSHT.	PROFILE
Identify the temporary physiological changes triggered by stress.	When faced with a perceived stressor, the body reacts physiologically to prepare itself for "fight or flight." These temporary physiological changes are designed to make people better able to defend themselves when a threat appears.	87	10-1	
Recognize the early warning signs of stress.	*Eustress* is a level of stress desirable for improved health and performance. When health and performance begin to suffer, the *distress* level has been reached. Early signs of distress can be recognized and, unless intervened against, may lead to more serious physical problems.			
		88	10-1	

OBJECTIVE	CONTENT SUMMARY	TRANSP.	LAB WKSHT.	PROFILE
Compute personal stress score.	The student stress scale provides a rough indication of stress levels based on life events.	89	10-1	
Recognize the potential of exercise as a stress management technique.	Physical activity that is enjoyable as play and in which competition is absent may help reduce the results of stress by using up the accumulated stress-related chemicals.		10-1	
Select stress management strategies and techniques that can best satisfy personal needs.	Stress can be controlled and reduced when the individual recognizes the causes, thus permitting the development of a plan to utilize appropriate strategies and techniques.	90	10-1	
Experiment with selected relaxation techniques.	Deep breathing, muscle relaxation, and meditative relaxation are presented as three methods for mastering the relaxation response.		10-1	

References

Benson, H. *The Relaxation Response.* New York: Avon, 1975.

Benson, H., and E. Stuart. *The Wellness Book.* New York: Simon & Schuster, 1993.

Consumer Reports Health Letter. "Stress Can Make You Sick." *Consumers Union* 2, no. 1 (January 1990): 1, 3, 4.

Goleman, D., and J. Gurin. *Mind Body Medicine.* Yonkers, NY: Consumer Reports Books, 1993.

Morgan, W. P., D. L. Costill, M. G. Flynn, J. S. Raglin, and P. J. O'Connor. "Mood Disturbance Following Increased Training in Swimmers." *Medical Science and Sports Exercise* 20 (1988): 408–14.

Selye, H. *Stress without Distress.* Philadelphia: J. B. Lippincott, 1974.

Tucker, L. "Exercise—One Way to Cope with Stress." *American Pharmacy* 19 (August 1979): 17.

University of California, Berkeley, Wellness Letter. "Healthy Lives: A New View of Stress." *University of California, Berkeley, Wellness Letter* 6, no. 9 (June 1990): 4–5.

11, 12, 13 — Exercising at Home or at a Fitness Facility, Programs for Special Needs, and Common Training Questions Answered

Chapter Guides

Chapters 11, 12, and 13 should serve as a resource to satisfy special student needs and interests. The instructor can selectively choose the content that is most appropriate.

OVERVIEW

OBJECTIVE	CONTENT SUMMARY	TRANSP.	LAB WKSHT.	PROFILE
Apply criteria for choosing commercial fitness facilities.	The selection of a commercial fitness facility should be made carefully after considering a number of critical factors.	91		
Recognize how exercise can be helpful in managing selected health problems.	Evidence indicates that exercise may help lower the blood pressure of those who are moderately hypertensive. Hypertensives will usually pursue a medically prescribed CRE program and tend to be cautious with regard to weight training.			

41

OBJECTIVE	CONTENT SUMMARY	TRANSP.	LAB WKSHT.	PROFILE
Identify ways to adapt physical activities to satisfy special needs.	Both Type 1 and Type 2 diabetics can benefit from a carefully prescribed and monitored CRE program. Exercise is often used to prevent and overcome orthopedic problems. Those with orthopedic limitations can often pursue fitness programs by adapting activities to their limitations.			
	Low-back pain is the most common orthopedic complaint, and once a diagnosis has been made, various lifestyle adjustments along with regular participation in exercise can usually hold the problem in check. Pre- and post-partum exercise programs have become popular and helpful.	92		
Recognize ways you can adjust to varied environments.	You can exercise in all weather conditions, provided that you dress accordingly and maintain fluid intake so that normal body temperature can be maintained.		13-1	
Recognize the effects of cigarettes on efforts to exercise.	Cigarette smoking can limit a person's capability to conduct aerobic activity.			
Identify ways to deal with common injuries and illnesses.	Most common injuries and illnesses can be dealt with and often prevented by implementing simple steps. The "RICE" principle is a means of dealing with acute injuries.	93 93		

References

Chapter 11

Goethel, P. "Medicine in the Fitness Center." *Fitness Management* 6, no. 5 (April 1990): 26-29.

Jordan, P., and H. Siegel. "Cued Access to Equipment." *Fitness Management* 6, no. 9 (August 1990): 24–29.

McClure, R. T. "Fitness in the Medical Center." *Fitness Management* 6, no. 5 (April 1990): 31–33.

Shephard, R. J. "Fitness Boom or Bust—A Canadian Perspective." *Research Quarterly of Exercise and Sport* 59 (1988): 265–69.

"The Skinning You Can Get at a Health Club." *Changing Times* 35 (September 1981): 64-66.

Stevens, T. "Secular Trends in Adult Physical Activity: Exercise Boom or Bust?" *Research Quarterly of Exercise and Sport* 58 (1987): 94–105.

Chapter 12

Block, L. *Low Back Pain —What It Is, What Can Be Done*. New York: Public Affairs Pamphlets, 1982.

Calliet, R. *Low Back Pain Syndrome*. 3rd. ed. Philadelphia: F. A. Davis Company, 1977.

Clarke, H. "Physical Activity during Menstruation and Pregnancy. *Physical Fitness Research Digest* 8 (July 1978): 1–25.

Cowan, M. M., and L. W. Gregory. "Responses of Pre- and Post-Menopausal Females to Aerobic Conditioning." *Medicine and Science in Sports and Exercise* 17 (1985): 138–43.

Daniels, L., and C. Worthingham. *Therapeutic Exercise*. 2nd. ed. Philadelphia: W. B. Saunders Company, 1977.

Erkkola, R. "The Influence of Physical Training During Pregnancy on Physical Work Capacity and Circulatory Parameters." *Scandinavian Journal of Clinical Laboratory Investigation* 36 (1976): 747.

Goldstein, D. "Clinical Applications for Exercise." *Physicians and Sportsmedicine* 17, no. 8 (1989): 82–93.

Ivy, J. "Exercise and Complications." *Diabetes Forecast* 43, no. 2 (1990): 46–49.

Kowal, M. A. "Review of Physiological Effects of Cryotherapy." *Journal of Orthopedics in Sports and Physical Therapy* 5 (1983): 66–73.

Kraus, H., A. Melleby, and S. Gaston. "Back Pain and Correction and Prevention." *New York State Journal of Medicine* 77 (1977): 1335–38.

Krzentowski, G., F. Pirnay, N. Pallikarakis, A. Luyckx, M. Lacroix, and P. Lefebvre. "Glucose Utilization during Exercise in Normal and Diabetic Subjects. The Role of Insulin." *Diabetes* 30 (1981): 983–89.

Lohmann, D., F. Liebold, W. Heilmann, H. Senger, and A. Pohl. "Diminished Insulin Response in Highly Trained Athletes." *Metabolism* 27 (1978): 521–24.

Macdonald, S., and P. Winfrey. "Back Basics." *Running and Fitness Newsletter* 8, no. 10 (Oct 1990): 4–5.

Marino, M. "Current Concepts on Rehabilitation in Sports Medicine." In: *The Lower Extremity and Spine in Sports Medicine*, J. Nicholas (ed.), pp. 142-52, St. Louis: Mosby, 1986.

Nirschl, R. P. "Tennis Elbow." *Journal of Bone and Joint Surgery* 61A (1979): 832–39.

Richter, E., N. Ruderman, and S. Schneider. "Diabetes and Exercise." *American Journal of Medicine* 70 (1981): 201–9.

Snyder-Mackler, L. "Rehabilitation of the Athlete with Low Back Pain." *Clinical Sports Medicine* 8 (1989): 717–29.

Taylor, P. M., and D. Taylor. *Conquering Athletic Injuries*. Champaign, IL: Human Kinetics Pub., 1988.

Chapter 13

American College of Sports Medicine. "Position Statement on Prevention of Heat Injuries During Distance Running." *Medicine and Science in Sports* 7 (1975): vii-ix.

Clement, D. B. "A Survey of Overuse Running Injuries." *Physician and Sportsmedicine* 9 (1981): 47.

Coyle, E. F., J. M. Hagberg, B. F. Hurley, W. H. Martin, A. A. Ehsani, and J. O. Holloszy. "Carbohydrate Feedings during Prolonged Strenuous Exercise Can Delay Fatigue." *Journal of Applied Physiology* 55 (1983): 230–35.

Drinkwater, B. L. "Physiological Responses of Women to Exercise." In: *Exercise and Sports Sciences Reviews*, Vol. 1, J. H. Wilmore (ed.), 126-154. New York: Academic Press, 1973.

Drinkwater, B. L., P. B. Raven, S. M. Horvath, J. A. Gliner, R. D. Ruhling, N. W. Boldran, and S. Taguchi. "Air Pollution, Exercise and Heat Stress." *Archives of Environmental Health* 28 (1974): 177–181.

Fleck, S. J., and J. E. Falkel. "Value of Resistive Training for the Reduction of Sports Injuries." *Sports Medicine* 3 (1986): 61–68.

Garrick, J. G., M.D. "Girls' Sports Injuries in High School Athletics." *Journal of the American Medical Association* 239, no. 21 (May 1978): 2245.

Halvorson, G. A. "Therapeutic Heat and Cold for Athletic Injuries." *Physician and Sportsmedicine* 18, no. 5 (May 1990): 87–94.

Haycock, C. E. "Susceptibility of Women Athletes to Injury— Myths vs. Reality." *Journal of the American Medical Association* 236, no. 2 (July 1976): 163.

Mirkin, G., and M. Hoffman. *The Sportsmedicine Book.* Boston: Little, Brown, 1978.

Nesbitt, L. "Runner's Knee—Chondromalacia Patellis." *Running and Fitness Newsletter* (May 1986): 6.

Owen, M. D., K. C. Kregel, T. Wall, and C. Gisolfi. "Effects of Ingesting Carbohydrate Beverages During Exercise in the Heat." *Medicine and Science in Sports and Exercise* 18 (1986): 568–75.

Kellett, J. "Acute Soft Tissue Injuries—A Review of the Literature. *Medicine and Science in Sports and Exercise* 18 (1986): 489.

Powell, K. E., H. W. Kohl, C. J. Caspersen, and S. N. Blair. "An Epidemiological Perspective of the Causes of Running Injuries. *Physician and Sportsmedicine* 14 (1986): 100–14.

Renstrom, P., and R. J. Johnson. "Overuse Injuries in Sports: A Review." *Sports Medicine* 2 (1985): 316.

Ryan, A. J., T. L. Bleiler, J. E. Center, and C. V. Gisolfi. "Gastric Emptying during Prolonged Cycling in the Heat. *Medicine and Science in Sports and Exercise* 21 (1989): 51–58.

Stamford, B. "How to Avoid Dehydration." *Physician and Sportsmedicine* 18, no. 7 (July 1990): 135-136.

Weltman, A., and B. Stamford. "Exercise and the Cigarette Smoker." *Physician and Sportsmedicine* 10 (December 1982): 153.

Wirth, V. "Running Through Pregnancy—Not Only Is It Safe, It May Save Your Life." *Runner's World* 13, no. 11 (November 1978): 55.

Wirth, V. "Running After Pregnancy—Positive Steps to Getting Back on Your Feet Fast." *Runner's World* 13, no. 12 (December 1978): 45.

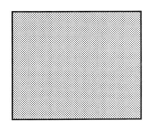

Lab Worksheets

LAB WORKSHEET 1-1

NAME_____SEC._____DATE_____

The Physical Fitness Continuum (Pages 3–4)

1. What level on the Physical Fitness Continuum best describes your status?

   _____

2. Where on the Physical Fitness Continuum would you like to be?

   _____

3. Check those factors listed below that may interfere with your achieving your desired place on the fitness continuum.

   _____ A. I can't find time to exercise regularly.

   _____ B. I am not clear about the right kind of exercise.

   _____ C. I have no one with whom to share my exercise.

   _____ D. I can't find an exercise program that I enjoy.

   _____ E. Physical or medical problems limit my exercise.

   _____ F. Other _____

LAB WORKSHEET 1-1 - CONTINUED

Guidelines for Medical Clearance (Pages 4–7)

4. Review the guidelines for medical clearance; check and complete the appropriate items below.

   _____ A. I should consult with my physician before starting up an exercise program because:_____

   _____

   _____

   _____ B. I believe that I can start an exercise program without consulting a physician.

Estimating Your Level of Activity (Page 8)

5. Complete Fitness Profile 1-1 and calculate your Activity Index to determine your estimated level of activity. Then check those items below that are most appropriate.

   _____ A. I am ready to increase my activity level.

   _____ B. I can safely take all fitness tests.

LAB WORKSHEET 1-2

NAME_____ SEC._____ DATE_____

The Five Components of Fitness (Pages 9–21)

1. Review Table 1-1, The Five Components of Physical Fitness; then alongside each of the components listed below, name a physical activity that you believe can influence the development of that component.

FITNESS COMPONENT	PHYSICAL ACTIVITY
Cardiorespiratory Endurance	_____
Body Composition	_____
Muscular Endurance	_____
Muscular Strength	_____
Flexibility	_____

Assessing Your Fitness (Pages 21–26)

2. Once you have completed your fitness assessment tests (Fitness Profiles 1-2 through 1-8), summarize the results on Fitness Profile 1-9. Review Fitness Profile 1-9 and list below, in priority order, those components that you would like to work on to improve your current fitness status (note the higher priority items first).

COMPONENT IMPROVEMENT LIST

1. _____
2. _____
3. _____
4. _____
5. _____

LAB WORKSHEET 1-2 - CONTINUED

Setting Goals (Pages 27–29)

3. Review Table 1-2 and select five fitness goals that you would most like to achieve. List them below.

FITNESS GOALS

A. _____

B. _____

C. _____

D. _____

E. _____

4. Note the components involved in the achievement of the goals that you have listed. How do they compare with those that you have noted in item 2 on this worksheet? If they are different, try to explain why.

_____

_____

_____

_____

LAB WORKSHEET 2-1

NAME_____SEC._____DATE_____

Progressive Overload (Pages 31–33)

1. Briefly explain how progressive overload can result in training effects. Your explanation should include the terms *increased demands* and *adaptation*.

   _____

   _____

   _____

Specificity (Pages 33–34)

2. For each of the fitness goals listed below, identify a fitness activity that you believe can effectively achieve that goal.

GOAL	FITNESS ACTIVITY
A. Improve fit of clothes	_____
B. Reduce discomfort from tension	_____
C. Reduce the chances of muscle or joint injury	_____
D. Reduce the risk of a circulatory system disorder	_____

Designing an Exercise Program (Pages 34–38)

3. Use other words to briefly describe each of the terms listed below:

   A. Exercise Intensity _____

   B. Exercise Duration _____

   C. Exercise Frequency _____

LAB WORKSHEET 2-1 - CONTINUED

4. In the next table, list one activity that you now do or have done in the past and note the intensity, duration, and frequency of your participation as well as one suggestion of how to provide progressive overload (note the example).

ACTIVITY	INTENSITY	DURATION	FREQUENCY	OVERLOAD
Example: walking	3 MPH	30 min.	5 times/wk	increase to 45 min.

LAB WORKSHEET 3-1

NAME_____ SEC._____ DATE_____

Aerobic and Anaerobic Activity (Pages 40–41)

1. List three ways that aerobic and anaerobic activities differ from one another, and provide one example of each type.

   _____

   _____

   _____

Cardiorespiratory Training Effects (Pages 44–45)

2. List two changes that might occur in your body if you improved your cardiorespiratory fitness.

   _____

   _____

The Risk Factors (Pages 45–48)

3. Use one of the terms *low*, *moderate*, or *high* to rate your vulnerability to each of the risk factors listed below. Briefly note one action step that you can take to reduce your vulnerability to any risk factor that you rated moderate or high.

RISK FACTOR	RATING	ACTION STEP
Hypertension		
Blood fat (cholesterol)		
Weight		
Smoking		
Stress		
Physical Inactivity		

LAB WORKSHEET 3-1 - CONTINUED

Aerobic Exercise Intensity–The Exercise Benefit Zone (Pages 52–56)

4. Review Table 3-1 and complete Fitness Profile 3-1; then note below the heart rate range that is correct for you during aerobic exercise.

          60% Est. MHR   85% Est. MHR

   60 sec._____   10 sec._____   60 sec._____   10 sec._____

Calories as a Measure of CRE Exercise (Pages 59–60)

5. Review Table 3-2 and note below the weekly calorie level that you would aim for to guide your CRE program.

    Calories used per week _____

6. Note the ideal workout duration and weekly frequency of your activities in order to achieve the calorie use level noted above.

    Duration of each workout _____

    Frequency each week _____

Exercise Systems and CRE (Pages 60–61)

7. How does Continuous Rhythmic Training differ from Interval Training?

_____

_____

_____

LAB WORKSHEET 4-1

NAME_____ SEC._____ DATE_____

Overweight, Overfat, and Obese (Pages 65–66)

1. Label each of the descriptions noted below using the most accurate of the following terms: overweight, overfat, or obese.

   A. A six-foot, large-framed man weighing 200 lbs. _____

   B. A female with 32% body fat _____

   C. A male with 30% body fat _____

Calories and Energy (Pages 66–67)

2. Label the type of calorie balance (neutral, negative, positive) described in each of the situations noted below.

   A. A daily food intake of 3000 calories and an exercise output of 2500:

   _____

   B. A daily food intake of 1500 calories and an exercise output of 2000:

   _____

   C. A daily food intake of 2000 calories and an exercise output of 2000:

   _____

3. What would the average daily negative calorie balance need to be if someone wanted to lose two pounds in two weeks? _____

4. Note the approximate number of pounds that would be lost in one year if you had a daily negative calorie balance of 100. _____

LAB WORKSHEET 4-1 - CONTINUED

Exercise and Diet (Pages 68–71)

5. Attempt to refute this statement:

   "You use so few calories during exercise that it is not practical to think that exercise can play a significant role in any program of weight control."

   _____

   _____

   _____

Choosing a Sensible Regimen (Pages 71–79)

6. Note three activities that you believe are very useful for controlling body composition.

   A. _____

   B. _____

   C. _____

7. What recommendation regarding exercise intensity, duration, and frequency would you have for someone interested in controlling his or her body composition?

   A. Intensity _____

   B. Duration _____

   C. Frequency _____

Note whether the statements that follow are TRUE or FALSE.

8. _____ All exercise tends to stimulate the appetite.

9. _____ "Spot reduction" is possible only if the correct type of exercise is selected.

LAB WORKSHEET 4-1 - CONTINUED

10. _____ If used correctly, rubber suits, vibrating machines, and saunas can help you lose body fat.

11. _____ Weight training has little to contribute to a program for controlling body composition.

12. _____ Exercise can help you to gain weight.

13. _____ Muscle turns to fat once an exercise program is discontinued.

LAB WORKSHEET 5-1

NAME_____ SEC._____ DATE_____

Differentiate Between Muscular Strength and Endurance (Pages 79–80)

1. Provide one example each of an activity that requires the use of:

   Muscular endurance _____

   Muscular strength _____

2. Identify two benefits of good muscular endurance and two benefits of good muscular strength.

   A. _____   B. _____

   A. _____   B. _____

How Muscles and Nerves Work Together (Page 80)

3. Briefly describe the working relationship of nerves, muscles, muscle fibers, and muscle units.

   _____

   _____

   _____

Atrophy and Hypertrophy (Pages 80–81)

4. What is the relationship between muscle use and disuse and the concepts of atrophy and hypertrophy?

   _____

   _____

   _____

LAB WORKSHEET 5-1 - CONTINUED

How Weight Training Develops Strength and Endurance (Pages 82–86)

5. Use the terms *resistance* and *repetitions* to describe the different approaches to developing muscular strength and endurance through the use of weight training.

_____

_____

_____

_____

Myths about Weight Training (Pages 86–88)

Note whether the statements that follow are TRUE or FALSE.

6. _____ Women should not weight train if they wish to avoid over-muscularization.

7. _____ Weight training has little use in programs designed to change body composition.

8. _____ Weight training should be avoided until one reaches adulthood and once one is in one's 50s or 60s.

9. _____ Weight training can increase bust size.

10. _____ Calisthenics are generally more useful for developing muscular endurance than muscular strength.

The Benefits of Good Flexibility (Pages 93–97)

11. Describe the benefits of a regular stretching program.

_____

_____

_____

LAB WORKSHEET 5-1 - CONTINUED

Ballistic and Static Stretching (Page 97)

12. Describe the difference between ballistic and static stretching, and indicate which is preferable and why.

   _____

   _____

   _____

   _____

LAB WORKSHEET 6-1

NAME_____SEC._____DATE_____

Select and Pursue Fitness Programs and Activities (Pages 98–156)

1. You will experiment with a variety of fitness programs and activities that you believe have the potential to help you achieve your personal fitness goals. Review the model programs and activities in Chapter 6 and Appendix B, and select those that you wish to try. Keep a record of your participation either on this worksheet or on a special progress card (i.e. calisthenic or interval circuit training progress card). Select activities for participation both at school and when you're away from school.

ACTIVITY	DATE								
Warm-up	(check)								
Stretching	(check)								
Walk/Jog/Run	(time)								
Weight Trng.	(check)								
Rope Skip	(check)								
Swimming	(check)								
Bicycling	(check)								
Other:	(check)								
Other:	(check)								
Other:	(check)								
Other:	(check)								

Lab Worksheets

LAB WORKSHEET 7-1

NAME_____SEC._____DATE_____

Getting Started and Keeping Going (Chapter 7)

1. Follow Steps 1 through 4 and complete Fitness Profile 7-1.

2. Follow Step 5; maintain a record of your program progress using either Fitness Profile 7-2 or 7-3 or both.

3. At the completion of two weeks on your program plan, respond to the following questions:

    A. How faithful are you to your contract commitment?

    _____

    _____

    B. If you are not compliant, why not? What can you do to become more consistent?

    _____

    _____

    _____

    C. When do you anticipate that it will be necessary to adjust your program plan? What adjustments will be made?

    _____

    _____

    _____

    D. What indications are there, if any, that you are achieving your goals?

    _____

    _____

LAB WORKSHEET 7-1 - CONTINUED

4. Look ahead to the future and speculate on your motivation to pursue a regular fitness program. What obstacles would you anticipate? How might you surmount these obstacles?

_____

_____

_____

LAB WORKSHEET 8-1

NAME_____ SEC._____ DATE_____

Essential Nutrients (Pages 174–179)

1. Alongside each of the essential nutrients listed below, note its general function and provide an example of a primary source.

NUTRIENTS	FUNCTION	SOURCE
Protein		
Carbohydrates		
Fats		
Vitamins		
Minerals		
Water		

Dietary Goals and Guidelines (Pages 179–180)

2. Review the dietary goals and guidelines on pages 179 and 180, then note below any changes that need to be made in your eating behavior to help you adhere to those goals and guidelines.

_____

_____

_____

_____

LAB WORKSHEET 8-1 - CONTINUED

The Daily Food Guide (Pages 180–182)

3. Provide an example of a dinner that contains each of the four food groups and that you would enjoy.

_____

_____

_____

Common Misconceptions (Pages 182–188)

Note whether the statements that follow are TRUE or FALSE.

4. _____ High cholesterol levels have been implicated as a primary risk factor in heart disease.

5. _____ Salt in your diet can help you maintain normal blood pressure levels.

6. _____ Sugar contains "empty calories."

7. _____ Caffeine is a stimulant.

8. _____ Most regular exercisers would be wise to use protein, vitamin, and mineral supplements, particularly if they wish to improve performance.

9. _____ Carbohydrate loading can be a beneficial practice for anyone participating in a road race.

10. _____ It is prudent to allow about three hours between eating and participating in an athletic event.

11. _____ A good way to keep your weight down is to sweat away excess weight.

12. _____ An alcoholic drink or two immediately prior to exercise can help you keep warm during cold weather.

LAB WORKSHEET 8-1 - CONTINUED

13. _____ Current recommendations are for the complete elimination of saturated fats from the diet.

14. _____ Tropical oils are unsaturated fats and should be included in one's daily diet.

15. _____ Fiber found in food has been linked to cancer and should be avoided.

LAB WORKSHEET 9-1

NAME_____ SEC._____ DATE_____

Model Weight Management Program (Pages 189–208)

1. Follow Steps 1 through 7 and complete Fitness Profiles 9-1A and 9-1B.

2. After completing two weeks of exercise and diet management, respond to the following questions:

   A. How faithful have you been to your contract commitment?

   _____

   _____

   B. If you are not compliant, why not?

   _____

   _____

   C. What can you do to become more compliant?

   _____

   _____

3. Note your "Common Eating Problems" from Step 7, and describe how you have been coping with them.

   _____

   _____

   _____

4. How have you changed your daily routine to increase calorie use beyond your regular exercise program?

   _____

   _____

LAB WORKSHEET 10-1

NAME_____ SEC._____ DATE_____

Identify Temporary Physiological Changes (Pages 210–211)

1. Check at least three temporary changes that you have experienced when faced with stressful situations.

    _____ rapidly beating heart

    _____ rapid and shallow breathing

    _____ muscles become tense

    _____ hands become cold

    _____ increase in perspiration

Recognize Early Warning Signs of Distress (Page 211)

2. From Table 10-1, list at least two signs from each category that you may have experienced.

    mood: _____

    _____

    internal: _____

    _____

    musculoskeletal: _____

    _____

Student Stress Scale (Page 213)

3. Using Table 10-2, calculate your stress score.

    _____

    _____

LAB WORKSHEET 10-1 - CONTINUED

Recognize Exercise as a Stress Management Technique (Pages 212–214)

4. Name at least one activity that causes you to feel more relaxed.

   _____

5. Describe the feelings you experience after participating in this activity.

   _____

   _____

   _____

Select Stress Management Strategies and Techniques to Best Satisfy Personal Needs (Pages 214–219)

6. Describe a situation that routinely causes you stress.

   _____

   _____

   _____

7. Select one technique from Table 10-3 that you believe may help you cope with this stress-inducing situation. Explain your choice.

   _____

   _____

   _____

   _____

LAB WORKSHEET 10-1 - CONTINUED

Experiment with Selected Relaxation Techniques (Pages 217–219)

8. Use the following ten-point scale to rate your tension before and after you do one of the three relaxation exercises described.

   1 = totally relaxed; no tension
   2 = very relaxed
   3 = moderately relaxed
   4 = fairly relaxed
   5 = slightly relaxed

   6 = slightly tense
   7 = fairly tense
   8 = moderately tense
   9 = very tense
   10 = extremely tense (the most uncomfortable you could be)

	BEFORE SESSION	AFTER SESSION	TECHNIQUE & COMMENTS
Monday			
Tuesday			
Wednesday			
Thursday			
Friday			
Saturday			
Sunday			

LAB WORKSHEET 13-1

NAME_____ SEC._____ DATE_____

Common Training Questions Answered (Chapter 13)

Note whether the statements that follow are TRUE or FALSE.

_____ 1. Heat stroke can be recognized by increased sweating.

_____ 2. It can be harmful to drink cold liquids when overheated from exercise.

_____ 3. It is best to avoid exercising when one has blisters.

_____ 4. A dry, clean environment is the best preventative for athlete's foot.

_____ 5. Rest and stretching is the best approach to treating tendinitis.

_____ 6. The application of heat is an important initial step when treating a sprained ankle.

_____ 7. Older athletes seem able to delay the aging process better than sedentary people do.

_____ 8. When comparing the strength, endurance, and body composition of large groups of male and female athletes, there are few actual differences between the fittest females and the fittest males.

_____ 9. Vigorous exercise should be avoided while menstruating.

_____ 10. The healing process for injuries that produce swelling can be helped by the immediate application of heat.

Fitness Profiles

YOUR FITNESS PROFILE 1-1
Calculating Your Activity Index

Objective: To determine your activity index on the basis of how hard, how long, and how often you exercise.

Directions: Rate the intensity, duration, and frequency of your current exercise patterns according to the criteria listed in the table. Then calculate your activity index, using the formula at the end of the table (intensity × duration × frequency = activity index). Suppose you are a skilled tennis player. Your intensity score for competitive singles would be 4; if the match lasts for an hour or more each time, your duration score would be 5; if you play regularly twice a week, your frequency score would be 2. Multiply 4 × 5 × 2 to get your activity index of 40 (moderate active). If, however, your exercise is limited to playing table tennis twice a week, your index would be 20 (2 × 5 × 2), or low active.

Rating: Your intensity _____ × your duration _____ × your frequency _____ = your activity index _____.

Assessing your activity index: Here's how you can translate your activity index into your estimated level of activity.

If your activity index is:	Your estimated level of activity is:
Less than 15	Sedentary
15–24	Low active
25–40	Moderate active
41–60	Active
Over 60	High active

Intensity: How Hard Do You Exercise?

If your exercise results in:	*Your intensity score is:*
No change in pulse from resting level	0
Little change in pulse from resting level—as in slow walking, bowling, yoga	1
Slight increase in pulse and breathing—as in table tennis, active golf (no golf cart)	2
Moderate increase in pulse and breathing—as in leisurely bicycling, easy continuous swimming, rapid walking	3
Intermittent heavy breathing and sweating—as in tennis singles, basketball, squash	4
Sustained heavy breathing and sweating—as in jogging, cross-country skiing, rope skipping	5

Duration: How Long Do You Exercise?

If each session continues for:	*Your duration score is:*
Less than 5 minutes	0
5 to 14 minutes	1
15 to 29 minutes	2
30 to 44 minutes	3
45 to 59 minutes	4
60 minutes or more	5

Frequency: How Often Do You Exercise?

If you exercise:	*Your frequency score is:*
Less than 1 time a week	0
1 time a week	1
2 times a week	2
3 times a week	3
4 times a week	4
5 or more times a week	5

Intensity × Duration × Frequency = Activity Index

YOUR FITNESS PROFILE 1-2
Taking the Modified Step Test

Objective: To complete 3 minutes of stepping at 24 steps per minute. *Warning:* If you have pain under or around your knee caps, it is probably not a good idea to take a step test. The step test, or climbing up and down stairs, can result in excessive compression on the underside of the knee cap and cause pain. Check with your doctor if you are unsure of the safety of this test for someone with your knee condition.

Directions:

1. Ask someone with a stopwatch or sweep-second hand to time you.
2. At the signal to begin, step up (start with either foot) on a stair or bench that is 8 inches from ground level and then step down again. Continue stepping up and down, alternating feet, for three consecutive minutes at a rate of 24 steps per minute—about 2 steps every five seconds. (A metronome can help you maintain the rhythm.)
3. Stop at exactly three minutes, and immediately sit in a chair. The active part of the test is now completed.
4. At exactly one minute after you complete the test, count your pulse for thirty seconds (see Chapter 3 for pulse-counting instructions) and multiply by 2 to obtain your one-minute pulse recovery score.
5. Determine the rating for your score by consulting the table "Heart Beats per Minute." If you are unable to step for the full three minutes, consider yourself very low in CRE.

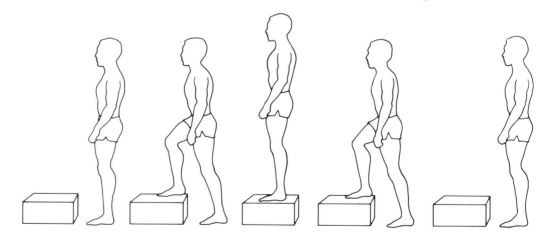

Rating: The scores in the table are for heartbeats per minute, measured 1 minute after completion of the modified step test.

Your score: _____.

Heart Beats per Minute					
Age	Very high	High	Moderate	Low	Very low
Female					
10–19	Below 82	82–90	92–96	98–102	Above 102
20–29	Below 82	82–86	88–92	94–98	Above 98
30–39	Below 82	82–88	90–94	96–98	Above 98
40–49	Below 82	82–86	88–96	98–102	Above 102
Over 50	Below 86	86–92	94–98	100–104	Above 104
Male					
10–19	Below 72	72–76	78–82	84–88	Above 88
20–29	Below 72	72–78	80–84	86–92	Above 92
30–39	Below 76	76–80	82–86	88–92	Above 92
40–49	Below 78	78–82	84–88	90–94	Above 94
Over 50	Below 80	80–84	86–90	92–96	Above 96

Assessing your modified step test score: If you are sedentary, your score will probably be around 100 or above, no matter what your age. Conversely, if you're exceptionally fit, your score will be below that of someone your age who is less fit. If your score on the modified step test is well below 100—falling within the very high or high rating—you have high CRE. Chances are you regularly do some activity that enhances CRE. Keep it up. A moderate or low rating indicates there is room for improvement in CRE. If your score falls within the very low rating, then a regular CRE program could make a big difference. Chapter 3 can help you plan a program to increase your CRE, should you so choose. To determine how you're progressing on a CRE program, you may want to use the modified step test on a regular basis. If so, remember to test yourself in the same way and under the same conditions (in the same general health, at the same time of day, at the same interval before or after a meal or vigorous activity, etc.).

Fitness Profiles

YOUR FITNESS PROFILE 1-3
Taking the 1.5-Mile Run-Walk Test

Objective: To run, walk, or run-walk a distance of 1.5 miles as quickly as possible. *Warning:* Do not take this test if you are ill or have significant risk factors that predispose you to coronary heart disease (i.e., smoking, obesity, high blood pressure, high blood fats, etc.) without checking with your doctor.

Directions:

1. Locate a running track or other area that provides exact measurements of up to 1.5 miles.
2. Have available a stopwatch or a clock with a clearly visible sweep-second hand.
3. Try to cover the distance at a pace that is best for you. Practice your pacing prior to taking the test to avoid going too fast at the outset and becoming prematurely fatigued. It could be helpful to review the model walk-jog programs in Chapter 6 for suggestions on pacing.
4. Avoid strenuous activity on the day of the test.
5. Avoid heavy eating or smoking for up to 3 hours before taking the test.
6. Avoid taking the test under extreme conditions of heat or cold, particularly if you have not been exercising under those conditions.
7. Warm up before taking the test (see pp. 134–137).
8. Cool down after the test (see pp. 134–137).
9. If possible have someone call out your time at various intervals of the test to determine whether your pace is correct.

Rating: In the table, find your age category and the time (in minutes and seconds) it took you to complete the 1.5-mile course.

Your time: _____.

1.5-Mile Run-Walk Test Ratings

Age	Superior	Excellent	Good	Fair	Poor	Very poor
Female						
13–19	Below 11:50	12:29–11:50	14:30–12:30	16:54–14:31	18:30–16:55	Over 18:31
20–29	Below 12:30	13:30–12:30	15:54–13:31	18:30–15:55	19:00–18:31	Over 19:01
30–39	Below 13:00	14:30–13:00	16:30–14:31	19:00–16:31	19:30–19:01	Over 19:31
40–49	Below 13:45	15:55–13:45	17:30–15:56	19:30–17:31	20:00–19:31	Over 20:01
Over 50	Below 14:30	16:30–14:30	19:00–16:31	20:00–19:01	20:30–20:01	Over 20:31
Male						
13–19	Below 8:37	8:37–9:40	9:41–10:48	10:49–12:10	12:11–15:30	Over 15:31
20–29	Below 9:45	9:45–10:45	10:46–12:00	12:01–14:00	14:01–16:00	Over 16:01
30–39	Below 10:00	10:00–11:00	11:01–12:30	12:31–14:45	14:44–16:30	Over 16:31
40–49	Below 10:30	10:30–11:30	11:31–13:00	13:01–15:35	15:36–17:30	Over 17:31
Over 50	Below 11:00	11:00–12:30	12:31–14:30	14:31–17:00	17:01–19:00	Over 19:01

YOUR FITNESS PROFILE 1-4
Determining Your Body Build

Objective: To determine your body build by measuring your wrist.

Directions: Measure the circumference of your wrist. One easy way to do this is to wrap a string around your wrist and then measure the length against a ruler.

Body Build Measurements

	Small	*Medium*	*Large*
Female	5.5 inches or less	5.6–6.2 inches	6.3 inches or more
Male	6.7 inches or less	6.8–7.4 inches	7.5 inches or more

Rating: Find your measurement on the table above. Determining your body build will help you use the height-weight chart in Appendix A.

Your measurement: _____.

YOUR FITNESS PROFILE 1-5
Methods for Assessing Body Composition

Using Skinfold Calipers

Objective: To accurately measure the amount of fat located under the skin.

Directions:

1. Have someone trained in the use of skinfold calipers measure you.
2. Take each measurement on the right side of the body.
3. Pinch a fold of skin between the thumb and forefinger. Do not include any muscle tissue in your grasp.
4. Place the contact surfaces of the calipers about ¼ inch below the tips of the pinching fingers.
5. While pinching the skin, permit the contact surfaces to close slowly to ensure that enough pressure is exerted to hold the skinfold.
6. Take readings to the nearest half millimeter.
7. Repeat the measurements until two consecutive measurements match.
8. Skinfold sites for women:
   a. *Suprailiac:* Pinch the skinfold at an angle above the right hip bone.

   Your measurement _____.

   b. *Triceps:* Pinch a vertical skinfold on the back of the arm midway between the shoulder and elbow. Your arm should hang naturally at your side.

   Your measurement _____.

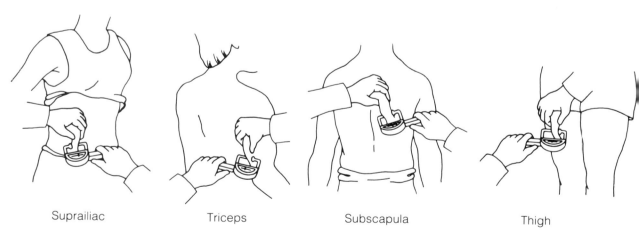

Suprailiac   Triceps   Subscapula   Thigh

76

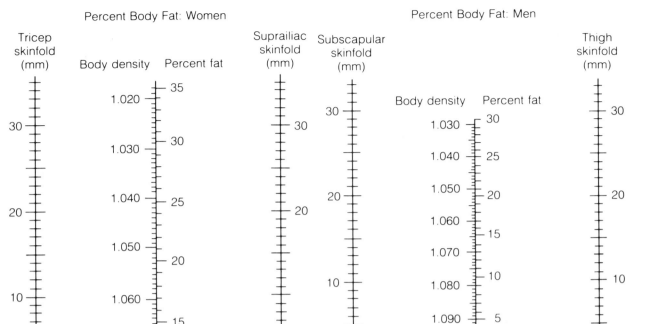

9. Skinfold sites for men:
   a. *Subscapula:* Pinch a diagonal fold just below the lower angle of the right scapula.

   Your measurement _____.

   b. *Thigh:* Pinch a vertical fold midway between the topmost point of the hip bone and the knee cap.

   Your measurement _____.

10. Mark each of your skinfold measurements on the appropriate "percent of body fat" chart. Connect the two marks with a straight line. Read your percent body fat on the middle scale.

Rating: Find your percentage of body fat in the table "Interpreting Body Fat Percentages."

Your percentage: _____.

Interpreting Body Fat Percentages		
	Men (%)	Women (%)
Obese	25 and higher	35 and higher
High fat	20–24	30–34
Above average	17–19	25–29
Average	13–16	20–24
Below average	10–12	17–19
Low fat	Below 10	Below 17

(*continued*)

YOUR FITNESS PROFILE 1-5
Methods for Assessing Body Composition (*continued*)

Body Mass Index

Body mass index (BMI) is a rough measure of body composition. This is a particularly good technique if your only tools for determining body fat are a bathroom scale to measure weight and a tape to measure height. It is a variance of the height-weight table and is based on the concept that a person's weight should be proportional to height. Although this technique has several weaknesses, it is fairly accurate for individuals who do not have an excessive amount of muscle mass.

Objective: To determine proportion of body fat according to individual height. Please note that BMI is not a measure of percent of body fat.

Directions: Using the following chart, place a ruler or other straight edge between the body weight column on the left and the height column on the right and read the BMI from the point where it crosses the center. In the example provided, a 190-pound woman, 65 inches tall (5 foot, 5 inches) would be on the borderline between overweight and obese, with a BMI of 29.5.

Body Mass Index (BMI)

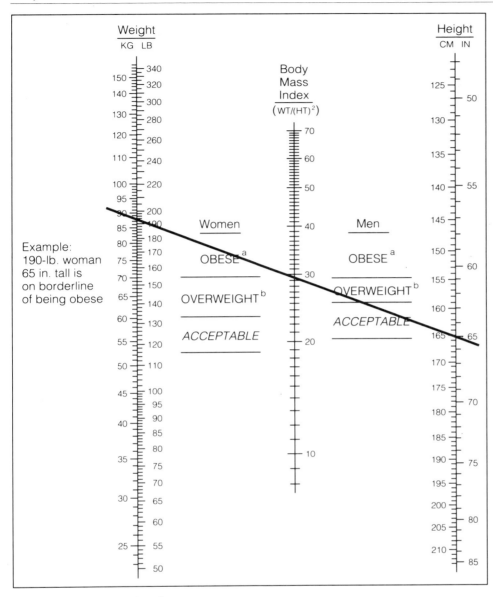

[a] *Obesity:* BMI above 30 kg/m².
[b] *Overweight:* Body mass index (BMI) of 25 to 30 kg/m².
SOURCE: Reprinted with permission from G. A. Bray, 1978, Definitions, measurements and classification of the syndrome of obesity, *International Journal of Obesity* 2:99–112.

Ideal body mass index:

Men should be less than 27.2.
Women should be less than 26.9.

YOUR FITNESS PROFILE 1-6
Taking the Grip-Strength Dynamometer Test

Objective: To assess your grip strength by using a hand dynamometer.

Directions: Hold the dynamometer in one hand (preferably the hand you write with). Squeeze the device as hard as you can; then read your score in pounds (or kilograms) on the dial. Consult the table "Grip Strength" for an interpretation of your grip score. The scores are given in pounds.

Rating: Because there is usually some change in body composition with increased age, scores should be adjusted to reflect an age-related decrease in the ratio of muscle to fat. People over age 50 should, therefore, add about 10 percent to their score.

Your score: _____.

Assessing your grip-strength score: If your score falls within the low or very low rating on the grip test, your overall muscular strength is probably also low or very low. If you choose to improve muscular strength by undertaking a specific exercise program, you are likely to see a dramatic improvement over time in your performance in activities requiring muscular strength. (See Chapter 5 for advice on planning an exercise program in this area.)

Grip Strength (in Pounds)					
	Very high	*High*	*Moderate*	*Low*	*Very low*
Female	Above 89	83–89	56–82	49–55	Below 49
Male	Above 154	136–154	105–135	91–104	Below 91

YOUR FITNESS PROFILE 1-7
Testing Your Muscular Endurance

Objective: To complete as many sit-ups in 60 seconds as possible and to complete as many push-ups or modified push-ups as you possibly can.

Directions:

1. *60-second sit-up* (Note: Don't try this if you have back trouble.): Start with your back flat on the floor and knees bent, feet flat on floor, arms crossed at chest. With feet held down (you'll need someone to assist), perform as many sit-ups as possible in 60 seconds. Touch elbows to your knees or thighs and return to the full starting position each time.

2. *Push-up:* Start in push-up position with arms straight, fingers forward. Lower chest to floor with back straight; then return to starting position. (Note: Many people may have insufficient strength to perform even a single push-up when using the push-up technique described here. The modified push-up allows such people to support themselves with their knees, thus reducing the need for upper-body strength in a test of muscular endurance.)

2a. *Modified push-up:* Same as push-up, except that you support yourself with your knees and keep your back straight.

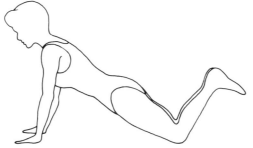

(continued)

YOUR FITNESS PROFILE 1-7
Testing Your Muscular Endurance (continued)

Ratings: Your scores are the maximum number of correct sit-ups in 60 seconds and the number of push-ups performed in succession. See the accompanying tables.

Your score for the 60-second sit-up test: _____.

Your score for the push-up or modified push-up test: _____.

Assessing your sit-up test score: This test measures muscular endurance of the abdominal muscles. You can improve a low or very low score by selecting weight training exercises for these muscles.

Assessing your push-up test score: This test evaluates the muscular endurance of your shoulder, arm, and chest muscles. You can improve a low or very low score by weight training exercises for these muscles.

Ratings for 60-Second Sit-up Test

Age	Very high	High	Moderate	Low	Very low
Female					
15–29	Above 43	39–43	33–38	29–32	Below 29
30–39	Above 35	31–35	25–30	21–24	Below 21
40–49	Above 30	26–30	19–25	16–18	Below 16
Over 50	Above 25	21–25	15–20	11–14	Below 11
Male					
15–29	Above 47	43–47	37–42	33–36	Below 33
30–39	Above 39	35–39	29–34	25–28	Below 25
40–49	Above 34	30–34	24–29	20–23	Below 20
Over 50	Above 29	25–29	19–24	15–18	Below 15

Ratings for Push-up and Modified Push-up Tests

Age	Very high	High	Moderate	Low	Very low
Push-up					
15–29	Above 54	45–54	35–44	20–34	Below 20
30–39	Above 44	35–44	25–34	15–24	Below 15
40–49	Above 39	30–39	20–29	12–19	Below 12
Over 50	Above 34	25–34	15–24	8–14	Below 8
Modified push-up					
15–29	Above 48	34–48	17–33	6–16	Below 6
30–39	Above 39	25–39	12–24	4–11	Below 4
40–49	Above 34	20–34	8–19	3–7	Below 3
Over 50	Above 29	15–29	6–14	2–5	Below 2

YOUR FITNESS PROFILE 1-8
Testing Your Trunk Flexibility

Objective: To reach as far forward as possible while sitting with your knees straight.

Directions: Before beginning this test, do some warm-up stretching exercises, such as bending sideways, forward, and backward several times, and rotating your trunk. Warm-ups may not only make it easier to perform the test, they may also help prevent strain or injury. In doing this test and the warm-ups that precede it, make your movements slow and gradual—never fast or jerky. Once warmed up, follow the procedure described below to test your trunk flexibility.

1. Place a box on the floor against a wall.
2. Tape a ruler on the box so that the 4-inch mark is on line with the near edge of the box and the 12-inch mark is farthest from you at the wall end of the box.
3. Sit on the floor with your legs extended so that your heels are about 5 inches apart and your feet are flat against the box.
4. Slowly reach with both hands as far forward as possible. Touch your fingertips to the yardstick and hold this position for about three seconds. Check the yardstick and note the distance you have reached.
5. Try this three times. (Do not attempt to add length by jerking forward.) Your flexibility score is the best of three trials.

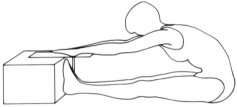

Rating: The scores in the "Trunk Flexibility" table are for the number of inches you reached.

Your score: _____ .

Trunk Flexibility (in Inches)					
	Very high	*High*	*Moderate*	*Low*	*Very low*
Female	Above 12	10–11	6–9	2–5	Below 2
Male	Above 11	8–10	3–7	1–2	Below 1

Assessing Your Trunk Flexibility Test Score: Although this test is a fair estimate of general flexibility for most people, it does not allow for differences in arm and leg length. Individuals with poor trunk flexibility could attain a good score on the test if they have long arms and short legs. Likewise individuals with short arms and long legs would attain poor scores. Women tend to be more flexible than men, as reflected in the scores listed. If your score on the trunk flexibility test falls within the low or very low rating and you cannot attribute this to short arms or long legs, then you may want to regularly do some of the various hamstring-stretching exercises suggested in the stretching model program in Chapter 6.

YOUR FITNESS PROFILE 1-9
A Summary of Your Fitness

Objective: To summarize the results of the physical fitness self-assessment tests in this chapter.

Directions: After completing Profiles 1-1, 1-2, 1-3, 1-5, 1-6, 1-7, and 1-8, fill in this worksheet to get a rough estimate of how you rate in each of the five components of physical fitness. The comments column provides space for noting any areas that need improvement.

Components of Physical Fitness

Activity index: _____ Estimated level of activity: _____

Components and tests	Results	Rating	Comments
Cardiorespiratory endurance			
Modified step test	_____	_____	_____
1.5-mile run-walk	_____	_____	_____
Body composition Percentage body fat	_____	_____	_____
Pinch test (p. 16)	_____	N/A	_____
Mirror test (p. 16)	_____	N/A	_____
BMI	_____	_____	_____
Muscular strength Grip strength	_____	_____	_____
Muscular endurance 60-second sit-up	_____	_____	_____
Push-up	_____	_____	_____
Modified push-up	_____	_____	_____
Flexibility Trunk flexibility	_____	_____	_____

YOUR FITNESS PROFILE 3-1
Computing Your Exercise Benefit Zone

Objective: To determine your exercise benefit zone.

Directions: Compute your predicted maximum heart rate per minute (HRM) by subtracting your age from 220. Then multiply your estimated HRM by .60 and .85. The result is called the exercise benefit zone (EBZ). Because during exercise you will count your own pulse rate for just 10 seconds, it is helpful to know your minimum and maximum "10-second conversion" EBZs. To compute it, divide your minimum and maximum EBZs by 6.

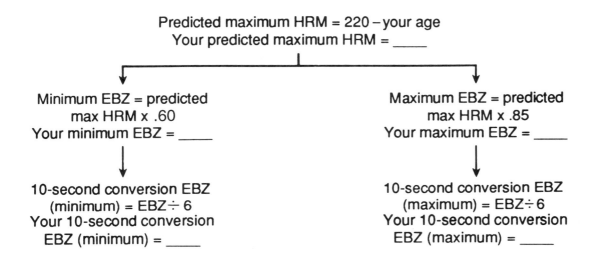

YOUR FITNESS PROFILE 4-1
Estimated Calorie Costs of Your Fitness Activities

Objective: To calculate how many calories you use per week doing fitness activities.

Directions: The table lists calorie costs for a sampling of fitness activities included in Appendix B. The second column shows estimated costs of calories per minute per pound of body weight. Multiply your body weight by the figure in the second column to get your estimated calorie cost per minute for an exercise or activity. (Turn to Appendix B for other activities.) To determine the number of calories you expend each week in a fitness activity, multiply this figure by the number of minutes you engage in the activity in a week.

Calorie Cost for Selected Fitness Activities				
Activity	Cal./min./lb.	× body weight	× min.	= Activity cal.
Aerobic dance (vigorous)	.062			
Basketball (vigorous, full court)	.097			
Bicycling (13 mph)	.071			
Canoeing (flat water, 4 mph)	.045			
Cross-country skiing (8 mph)	.104			
Handball (skilled, singles)	.078			
Horseback riding (trot)	.052			
Jogging (5 mph)	.060			
Rowing (vigorous)	.097			
Running (8 mph)	.104			
Soccer (vigorous)	.097			
Swimming (55 yds./min.)	.088			
Table tennis (skilled)	.045			
Tennis (beginner)	.032			
Walking (4.5 mph)	.048			
Other (from App. B or Model Programs)	___			
Other	___			
Other	___			
Total per week				

Rating: Estimated calories you expend in fitness activities per week: _____.

YOUR FITNESS PROFILE 4-2
Estimated Calorie Costs of Your Nonsport Activities

Objective: To calculate how many calories you use each week doing nonsport activities.

Directions: This table lists calorie costs for a sampling of nonsport activities. The second column shows estimated costs of calories per minute per pound of body weight. Multiply your body weight by the figure in the second column to get your estimated calorie cost per minute for an activity. To determine the number of calories you expend each week in a nonsport activity, multiply this figure by the number of minutes you engage in the activity in a week.

Calorie Cost for Selected Nonsport Activities				
Activity	*Cal./min./lb.*	× *body weight*	× *min.*	= *Activity cal.*
Bathing, dressing, undressing	.021	_____	_____	_____
Bed-making (and stripping)	.031	_____	_____	_____
Chopping wood	.049	_____	_____	_____
Cleaning windows	.024	_____	_____	_____
Driving a car	.020	_____	_____	_____
Gardening				
Digging	.062	_____	_____	_____
Hedging	.034	_____	_____	_____
Raking	.024	_____	_____	_____
Weeding	.038	_____	_____	_____
Ironing	.029	_____	_____	_____
Kneading dough	.023	_____	_____	_____
Laundry (taking out and hanging)	.027	_____	_____	_____
Mopping floors	.024	_____	_____	_____
Painting house (outside)	.034	_____	_____	_____
Plastering walls	.023	_____	_____	_____
Sawing wood (crosscut saw)	.058	_____	_____	_____
Shoveling snow	.052	_____	_____	_____
Other (estimate from above)	____	_____	_____	_____
Other	____	_____	_____	_____
Other	____	_____	_____	_____
Total per week				

Rating: Estimated calories you expend in nonsport activities per week: _____.

YOUR FITNESS PROFILE 4-3
Estimated Calorie Costs of Your Sedentary Activities

Objective: To calculate how many calories you expend weekly in sedentary activities.

Directions: The table lists calorie costs for a sampling of sedentary activities. The second column shows estimated costs of calories per minute per pound of body weight. Multiply your body weight by the figure in the second column to get your estimated calorie cost per minute for an activity. To determine the number of calories you expend each week in a sedentary activity, multiply this figure by the number of minutes you engage in the activity in a week.

Calorie Cost for Selected Sedentary Activities				
Activity	*Cal./min./lb.*	× *body weight*	× *min.*	= *Activity cal.*
Card playing	.012	_____	_____	_____
Eating (sitting)	.011	_____	_____	_____
Knitting and sewing	.011	_____	_____	_____
Piano playing	.018	_____	_____	_____
Sitting quietly	.009	_____	_____	_____
Sleeping and resting	.008	_____	_____	_____
Standing quietly	.012	_____	_____	_____
Typing (electric)	.013	_____	_____	_____
Writing	.013	_____	_____	_____
Other (estimate additional sedentary activities guided by the above list)	____	_____	_____	_____
Other	____	_____	_____	_____
Other	____	_____	_____	_____
Total per week				

Rating: Estimated calories you expend in sedentary activities per week: _____.

YOUR FITNESS PROFILE 5-1
Determining Your Normal Range of Joint Motion

Objective: To estimate the flexibility and range of motion in your major joints.

Directions: Illustrated here is the normal range of motion for some of the major joints. By comparing the motion of your joints with the illustrations, you should be able to determine whether you have normal range. The approximate degree of movement is noted on each illustration. If any one of your joints has a limited range, see the stretching model program in Chapter 6. If you decide to try to increase your range of motion, remember that for most people there is no need to achieve flexibility beyond normal range.

1. Raise and lower your arm at the shoulder, sideward.

   ___ Range OK

   ___ Needs Improvement

   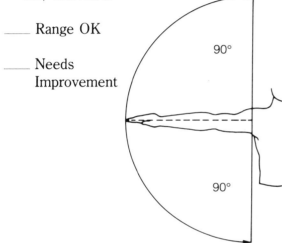

2. Turn your shoulder, palm outward and palm inward.

   ___ Range OK

   ___ Needs Improvement

   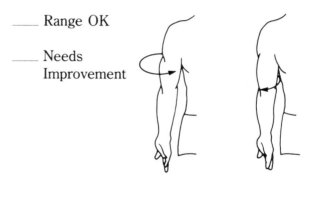

3. Raise and lower your arm at the shoulder, forward and to the rear.

   ___ Range OK

   ___ Needs Improvement

   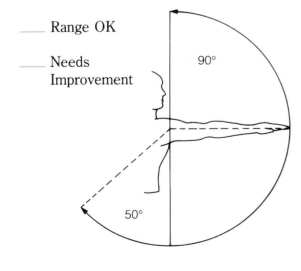

4. Turn your palm up and palm down.

   ___ Range OK

   ___ Needs Improvement

   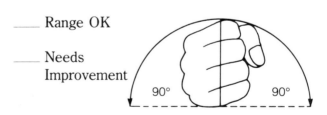

5. Bend and straighten your elbow.

   ____ Range OK

   ____ Needs Improvement

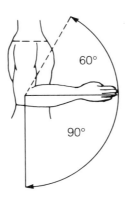

6. Raise leg to the side at the hip.

   ____ Range OK

   ____ Needs Improvement

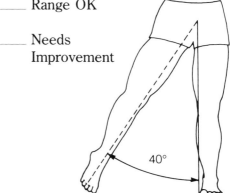

7. Raise and lower your leg forward at the hip.

   ____ Range OK

   ____ Needs Improvement

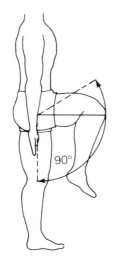

8. Bend and straighten your knee.

   ____ Range OK

   ____ Needs Improvement

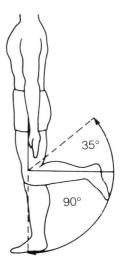

9. Raise and lower your foot at the ankle.

   ____ Range OK

   ____ Needs Improvement

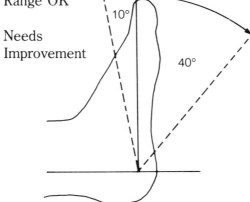

YOUR FITNESS PROFILE 7-1
Personal Fitness Contract

Objective: To help you make a more lasting commitment to your physical fitness.

Directions:

1. Fill in the specific goals you would like to achieve.
2. Place a check under the fitness components you need to develop to achieve each goal you selected. See Table 1-2 in Chapter 1 for help with this step.
3. Fill in the activities you have selected.
4. For each of the activities that you have selected, place a check under each of the components that you can develop as a result of regular participation in these activities. Table 1 in Appendix B or Chapter 7 will help to guide you through this step.
5. Check off your intended frequency and indicate duration.
6. Sign and date your contract in the presence of a witness who can help you maintain your commitment.
7. Have your witness sign the contract as well.

Personal Fitness Contract

I, _Katie Price_, am contracting with myself to follow an exercise program to achieve and work at the following fitness goals and components.

Fitness Goals (Note as many as appropriate.)	Fitness Components (Check as appropriate.)				
	CRE	BC	MS	ME	F
1. Prevent heart attack at an early age	✓				
2. Become more muscular; firm up		✓	✓	✓	
3. Prevent joint injury from athletics			✓		✓

Program Plan

Activities	Components (Check ✓)					Intensity	Duration	Frequency (Check ✓)						
	CRE*	BC*	MS	ME	F			M.	Tu.	W.	Th.	F.	Sa.	Su.
1. Jogging	✓	✓		✓		140-170	30 m	✓		✓		✓		
2. Weight training			✓	✓	✓	8-15	3 sets	✓		✓		✓		
3. Stretching					✓	Mod.	10 secs.	✓		✓		✓		✓
4.														
5.														

Personal Fitness Contract

I, _____, am contracting with myself to follow an exercise program to achieve and work at the following fitness goals and components.

Fitness Goals (Note as many as appropriate.)	Fitness Components (Check as appropriate.)				
	CRE	BC	MS	ME	F
1. _____					
2. _____					
3. _____					
4. _____					
5. _____					
6. _____					
7. _____					
8. _____					

Program Plan

Activities	Components (Check ✓)					Intensity	Duration	Frequency (Check ✓)						
	CRE*	BC*	MS	ME	F			M.	Tu.	W.	Th.	F.	Sa.	Su.
1. ____														
2. ____														
3. ____														
4. ____														
5. ____														
6. ____														
7. ____														
8. ____														
9. ____														
10. ____														

I will begin my program on _____ .

I agree to maintain a record of my activity, assess my progress periodically, and, if necessary, revise my goals.

Signed _____ Date _____

Witness _____

*You should conduct activities for achieving CRE and body composition goals at an intensity within your EBZ.

YOUR FITNESS PROFILE 7-2
Your Program Log

Objective: To summarize your overall fitness plan and record your follow-through.

Directions:

1. List all the activities in your program. Include those you plan to do outside of class.
2. Post the date, at the top of each column, for each day that you exercise.
3. Make the appropriate notation for each exercise. For aerobic activities, note the total exercise time. For activities achieving muscular goals, simply place a check under the appropriate date. You should place specific notations for such programs as circuit training or weight training on separate progress cards in addition to checking them off on this chart.

PROGRAM LOG

Name: Katie Price
Date: 9/24

Exercise program	10/1	10/2	10/3	10/4	10/5									
1. Jogging	20 m		20		20									
2. Weight Training	✓	✓		✓										
3. Bicycling		30 m		35										
4. Swimming		15 m		15										

Fitness Profiles

PROGRAM LOG

Name _____   Date _____

Exercise program											
1.											
2.											
3.											
4.											
5.											
6.											
7.											
8.											
9.											
10.											

YOUR FITNESS PROFILE 7-3
A Weekly Log for Your CRE Progress

Objective: To record your exercise time or distance as a way of marking your progress.

Directions: Use this progress chart to record the distance you cover or the time you spend each day of the week on a CRE activity. (You will find the weekly calorie count in Table 6-4, p. 105.) You can use this log to record progress for more than one activity.

CRE Progress Chart

Week	Activities	Mon.	Tues.	Wed.	Thur.	Fri.	Sat.	Sun.	Weekly distance or time	Weekly calorie cost
1	Walking	30 min.		30 min.		30 min.		30 min.	2 hrs.	468
2	Walking		30 min.	30 min.	30 min.		30 min.	30 min.	2 hrs. 30 min.	585
3	Walk/jog		35 min.	35 min.		35 min.		35 min.	2 hrs. 20 min.	882
4										
5										
6										
7										
8										
9										
10										
11										

CRE Progress Chart

Week	Activities	Mon.	Tues.	Wed.	Thur.	Fri.	Sat.	Sun.	Weekly distance or time	Weekly calorie cost

YOUR FITNESS PROFILE 9-1A
Identifying Weight-Loss and Negative-Calorie-Balance Goals
(When Percentage of Body Fat Is Known)

Objective: To set weight-loss and negative-calorie-balance goals.

Directions: Review pp. 17 and 18 in Chapter 1 to determine your current level of body fat and the extent to which you need to alter that percentage. Use the formulas below to calculate your ultimate target-weight and negative-calorie goals.

1. _____ = _____ − _____
   % body fat to be lost   % current body fat   Target % body fat

2. _____ = _____ × _____
   Pounds to lose   % body fat to be lost   Current weight

3. _____ = _____ − _____
   Target body weight   Current weight   Pounds to lose

4. _____ = _____ ÷ _____
   Number of weeks to   Total pounds to lose   Pounds to lose each week
   achieve target weight

5. _____ = _____ × 3,500
   Negative-calorie balance to   Pounds to lose each week
   achieve each week

YOUR FITNESS PROFILE 9-1B
Identifying Weight-Loss and Negative-Calorie-Balance Goals (Using Height-Weight Tables)

Objective: To set weight-loss and negative-calorie-balance goals.

Directions: Determine your body build using Profile 1-4 in Chapter 1. Then, using the height-weight tables in Appendix A, fill in the following formulas.

1. _____ = _____ − _____
   Pounds to lose   Current weight   Target weight (charts, p. 270)

2. _____ = _____ ÷ _____
   Number of weeks to   Total pounds to lose   Pounds to lose each week
   achieve target weight

3. _____ = _____ × 3,500
   Negative-calorie balance to   Pounds to lose each week
   achieve each week

YOUR FITNESS PROFILE 9-2
Calorie Intake Log

Objective: To make you aware of when, what, and how much you eat.

Directions:

1. Record the time of day that you eat the food in column 1.
2. Describe the food in column 2. Don't forget the details—the butter on the bread, the sugar in the coffee, and so on.
3. Note the amount of food you eat in column 3. This is usually noted by the general size or weight of the serving. See Appendix C for the serving designations and calorie equivalents of a large variety of foods.
4. Write the number of calories contained in a specific food serving in column 4. Appendix C lists the calorie costs of most foods by their exchange categories.
5. Include comments related to your mood or hunger level and other circumstances connected to food intake in column 5. For example, you might use words or comments such as "anxious," "very hungry," or "snack."
6. Calculate the total number of calories that you take in, and at the end of each day note the total on Profile 9-4 "Weekly Calorie Balance Form."

Daily Intake Log

1 Time	2 Food	3 Amount	4 Calories	5 Comments

Total calorie intake: _____.

YOUR FITNESS PROFILE 9-3
Calorie Output Log

Objective: To make you aware of how active or sedentary you are.

Directions:

1. Under the activity column, list all your physical activities for the day. For purposes of this worksheet, physical activity refers to all sport and fitness activities as well as other active movement that generates at least .02 calorie per pound per minute. You can find a partial listing of common nonsport activities that fit into this category in Profile 4-2 (in Chapter 4). It is not necessary to list your sedentary activities such as sleeping and eating; they burn less than .02 calorie per minute per pound and are lumped together in the sedentary activity category.
2. Place under column 2 the calorie cost per minute per pound for each of the physical activities you listed in the activity column. You will find the appropriate calorie costs for most of these activities in Profile 4-1 and Profile 4-2 in Chapter 4 and in Appendix B.
3. All your sedentary activities have been lumped together and assigned an average value of .01 calorie per minute per pound.
4. Place the total number of minutes of activity under column 3 alongside each of the physical activities listed.
5. Calculate the total number of minutes to place under column 3 alongside the sedentary category by adding up all the minutes of physical activity and subtracting the amount from 1,440 (the total number of minutes in a day).
6. Note your body weight under column 4 alongside each of the physical activities and the sedentary category.
7. To determine your total calorie output for each of the physical activities as well as for the sedentary activity, under column 5, you must multiply column 2 by column 3 by column 4.
8. To obtain your calorie output for the entire day, total all the figures under column 5.
9. You should note the total number of calories you burn each day on Profile 9-4, "Weekly Calorie Balance Form," If your logs of calorie intake and output are typical of your weekly pattern, a review of Profile 9-4 will enable you to assess whether you have a negative or positive calorie balance. It can also guide you in determining how to adjust that balance to reach a new negative balance.

Daily Output Log

1 Activity	2 Cal./min./lb.	×	3 Total minutes	×	4 Body weight	=	5 Output
1.		×		×		=	
2.		×		×		=	
3.		×		×		=	
4.		×		×		=	
5.							
6.							
7.							
8.							
Sedentary	.01	×		×		=	

Total calorie output: _____ .

YOUR FITNESS PROFILE 9-4
Weekly Calorie Balance Form

Objective: To make you aware of how many calories you use in the course of a week.

Directions: Insert in this profile the intake and output figures you gathered in Profiles 9-2 and 9-3.

Weekly Balance

	Sun.	Mon.	Tues.	Wed.	Thurs.	Fri.	Sat.
Calories in							
Calories out							
Daily difference							
Weekly difference							

Physical Activity Plan

Activities*	Session duration	Frequency (Check √)						
		M.	Tu.	W.	Th.	F.	Sa.	Su.
1.								
2.								
3.								
4.								
5.								
6.								
7.								

I will begin my program on _____.

I agree to maintain a record of my progress, and, if necessary, revise my goals.

Signed _____ Date _____

Witnessed by _____

*Conduct all activities at an intensity within the EBZ, although brisk walking and similar aerobic activities provide greatest calorie-burning effects as a result of durations of more than 30 minutes to over an hour, five times per week.

YOUR FITNESS PROFILE 9-5
A Personal Weight Control Contract

Objective: To draw up a personal contract for weight control.

Directions:

1. Review Table 1-2 in Chapter 1 to help you decide on the specific body composition goals you want to list in your contract.
2. Refer to Profile 9-1A or Profile 9-1B to determine your target weight, target date, and your weekly negative-calorie-balance goals.
3. Review Profiles 9-2, 9-3, and 9-4 to help you determine your calorie intake and output goals.
4. Consult the discussion on selecting a sport or activity (pp. 272–295) to help you decide on the physical activities that you want to commit yourself to in your contract. Once you have decided on specific activities, it is most useful to list the exercise intensity and duration as well as the specific days when you expect to participate in the activities.
5. Note the date you want to begin your program. Then sign your contract along with a witness, someone who can hold you accountable.

Weight Control Contract

I, _____, am contracting with myself to follow a weight control program of exercise and diet management to help me alter my body composition.

The body composition goals that I expect to achieve are:

1. _____
2. _____
3. _____
4. _____
5. _____

I expect to achieve a target weight of _____ lbs. by the target date of _____.

During this time, my weekly negative-calorie-balance goal is _____ calories.

My diet plan will include a daily food intake of _____ calories.

My exercise plan will include a daily output of _____ calories.

YOUR FITNESS PROFILE 9-6
Plan Your Weekly Menus

Objective: To devise a week's menus that maintain your nutritional balance and stay within your target calorie amounts.

Directions:

1. From Table 9-2, determine the portions of each food group that you are allowed, so you can meet your calorie intake goal. Table 9-2 shows allowable portions for calorie plans of 1,000, 1,200, 1,500, 1,800, and 2,100. See Table 9-3 to determine size of portion.
2. Select your specific foods from Appendix C, "Food Exchange Plan," and record them for each day of the week alongside the appropriate meal or snack. The beauty of the food exchange list is the limitless variety of menus that are possible.
3. Place the portion size alongside the listed food. You can obtain the portion size from Table 9-3, "Calories per Portion," or from Appendix C. It is important to adhere to the correct portion size; for example, if you prepare a three-ounce portion of meat, that would count as three meat exchanges.

Sample Daily Menu Planner

Date 9/16/87   Calories per day 1,800

Meal and Food Group		Portions	Menus
Breakfast	meat	1	½ grapefruit
	fat	1	1 poached egg
	bread	1	1 slice whole wheat toast, 1 tsp. diet margarine
	milk	0	tea or coffee
	veg.	0	
	fruit	1	
Snack	fat	0	1 glass skim milk
	bread	1	2 graham crackers
	milk	1	1 apple
	veg.	0	
	fruit	1	
Lunch	meat	2	4 oz. orange juice
	fat	1	2 oz. turkey on rye bread, tomato, lettuce,
	bread	2	and 1 tsp. mayonnaise
	milk	0	tea or coffee
	veg.	2	
	fruit	1	
Snack	fat	1	1 cup unflavored, low-fat yogurt
	bread	0	2 T. raisins
	milk	1	
	veg.	0	
	fruit	1	
Dinner	meat	4	4 oz. broiled flounder with ½ c. brown rice
	fat	2	½ c. broccoli, ½ c. carrots, sliced tomato
	bread	2	1 slice whole wheat bread with 1 tsp. margarine
	milk	0	¼ cantaloupe
	veg.	3	caffeine-free diet soda
	fruit	1	
Snack	fat	0	3 cups popcorn
	bread	1	celery
	milk	1	1 glass skim milk
	veg.	1	
	fruit	0	

Portions allowed each day: Meat 7 Fat 5 Bread 7 Milk 3 Veg. 6 Fruit 5

4. Study the partially filled-in weekly menu before using the blank worksheet. The example presents an 1,800-calorie plan. For variety, you may change the number of portions of various food groups.

Daily Menu Planner

Date _____   Calories per day _____

Meal and Food Group		Portions	Menus
Breakfast	meat fat bread milk veg. fruit		
Snack	fat bread milk veg. fruit		
Lunch	meat fat bread milk veg. fruit		
Snack	fat bread milk veg. fruit		
Dinner	meat fat bread milk veg. fruit		
Snack	fat bread milk veg. fruit		

Portions allowed each day: Meat _____ Fat _____ Bread _____ Milk _____ Veg. _____ Fruit _____

Fitness Profiles

YOUR FITNESS PROFILE 9-7
Weight Control Progress Graph

Objective: To chart your weight control progress to keep you on track.

Directions:

1. Note your starting weight on the graph.
2. Draw a dot under each week alongside the appropriate weight change. Place each dot in the center of the appropriate box.
3. Connect the dots from week to week. This will provide a graphic picture of your progress. It is not uncommon for a temporary rise in weight to occur occasionally, but the general trend should be downward. If it is not, you may have to decrease your calorie intake or increase your calorie output through physical activity. The solid line shows a gradual weight loss of one pound per week. If your dots are located along the line, you are losing at the rate of one pound per week. Below the line you will be losing at a more rapid rate and above the line at a slower rate.

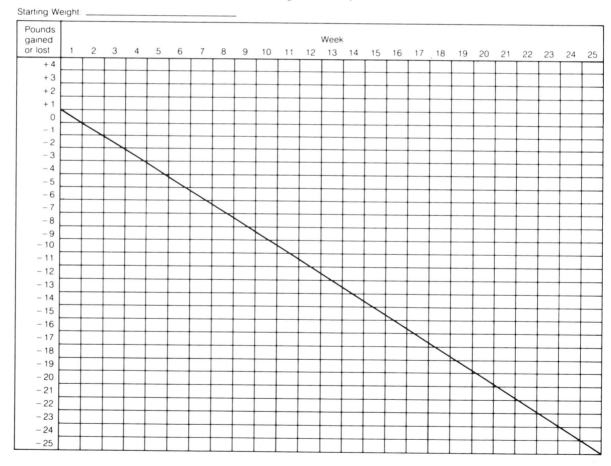

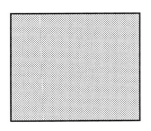

Examination Questions

CHAPTER 1

TRUE/FALSE

1. Body composition may be defined as the percentage of the body that is fat.

2. Muscular strength may be defined as the ability to repeat movements over and over.

3. Aerobic fitness is synonymous with cardiorespiratory endurance.

4. A person can be overweight without being overfat.

5. Men tend to be more flexible than women.

6. The components of health-related fitness include speed and balance.

7. Improving muscular endurance and flexibility may decrease soreness due to exercise.

8. Your activity index is based solely on the intensity of your workouts.

9. If you have no physical complaints, it is probably safe for you to begin an exercise program at your current level of activity and gradually increase it.

10. The "pinch test" is an extremely accurate way to assess body composition.

11. Your body weight is the best indication of your level of body fat.

12. Height and weight are necessary to calculate body mass index.

13. The best example of muscular endurance is lifting the heaviest weight possible.

14. Your physical activity index can be determined using the formula: *intensity × duration × frequency*.

15. Flexibility of a joint is measured by the range of motion of that joint.

16. An excess of fat round your waist may increase the risk to your health.

MULTIPLE CHOICE

17. It is safe to begin an exercise program if:
    a. you smoke cigarettes
    b. you have been sedentary for a number of years
    c. you start at your current level of fitness and gradually increase it
    d. you have had a medical checkup within the past five years

18. Cardiorespiratory endurance can *best* be defined as:
    a. the ability to do strenuous physical activity over a period of time, using maximum effort throughout
    b. having healthy circulatory and respiratory systems
    c. the ability to do physical activity without any increase in your heart rate
    d. the ability to do moderately strenuous activity over an extended period of time

19. Your body composition is *best* defined as:
    a. the percentage of your body that is fat
    b. your body weight
    c. the general shape of your body
    d. how well defined your musculature is

20. Shortness of breath following very quickly after physical activity most likely indicates limitations in:
    a. muscular endurance
    b. speed
    c. body composition
    d. cardiorespiratory endurance

21. Aerobic fitness is synonymous with:
    a. body composition
    b. cardiorespiratory endurance
    c. motor ability
    d. muscular strength

22. Which of the following matches the fitness component with the appropriate test?
    a. cardiorespiratory endurance; the modified step test
    b. muscular strength; biceps pinch test
    c. body composition; 1.5-mile run-walk test
    d. muscular strength; trunk flexion

23. Which of the following fitness goals would *least* likely be influenced by changes in body composition?
    a. reduction of low-back pain
    b. control of diabetes
    c. decreased muscle soreness due to physical activity
    d. a reduction in high blood pressure

24. Improved flexibility can help you to:
    a. prevent muscle and joint injuries
    b. improve the fit of your clothes
    c. prevent heart attacks
    d. lower cholesterol levels

25. Which of the following statements is most consistent with the concept of physical fitness?
    a. It is a precisely definable entity.
    b. It should follow fixed standards.
    c. It needs to be defined in accordance with an individual's special needs and interests.
    d. It is the same thing for everyone.

26. The concept of a physical fitness continuum:
    a. is useful only when applied to groups of individuals who are similar in age and athletic experience
    b. cannot be applied to people with medical problems
    c. can be applied to anyone no matter what their current level of physical fitness is
    d. represents a fixed standard to be applied in the same way for everyone

27. Medical clearance prior to starting a fitness program:
    a. is not necessary if you are under thirty-five
    b. is recommended if you have been sedentary for a long time
    c. is not necessary unless you have a history of any of the risk factors for coronary heart disease
    d. is not necessary unless you are feeling ill

28. The activity index in Profile 1-1 is designed:
    a. to help you determine whether it is safe for you to proceed to strenuous fitness tests
    b. to serve as a good estimate of your current fitness level
    c. to replace more strenuous fitness tests
    d. to be used only after you have received medical clearance to begin a fitness program

29. Your activity index is based solely on:
    a. the intensity of your workouts
    b. the frequency of your workouts
    c. the duration of your workouts
    d. your current exercise patterns over the past three months

30. Which of the following is *not* generally accepted as a component of health-related fitness?
    a. muscle coordination
    b. flexibility
    c. cardiorespiratory endurance
    d. muscular strength

31. Which of the following provides the *best* example of muscular strength?
    a. the ability to do many push-ups
    b. the ability to lift a heavy weight above your head
    c. the ability to run a long distance
    d. the ability to bring a joint through a wide range of movement

32. Which of the following fitness components is *best* exemplified by lifting a heavy weight over your head?
    a. muscular endurance
    b. muscular strength
    c. flexibility
    d. body composition

33. Difficulty in doing repeated push-ups usually indicates limitations in:
    a. flexibility
    b. muscular strength
    c. muscular endurance
    d. body composition

34. Difficulty in moving a joint through a full range of movement most likely indicates limitations in:
    a. flexibility
    b. muscular strength
    c. muscular endurance
    d. body composition

35. Flexibility is:
    a. the ability to do many push-ups
    b. the ability to exert a force against a resistance
    c. measured by the range of movement in a joint
    d. the ability to run a long distance

36. A good test of cardiorespiratory endurance is:
    a. a 60-second sit-up
    b. push-ups
    c. the modified step test
    d. the pinch test

37. Which of the following matches the fitness component with the appropriate test?
    a. cardiorespiratory endurance; sit-ups
    b. muscular strength; push-ups
    c. flexibility; skinfold test
    d. body composition; pinch test

38. Which fitness component would you be most likely to work on if you wanted to lower your resting heart rate?
    a. cardiorespiratory endurance
    b. body composition
    c. muscular strength
    d. muscular endurance

39. Which component would you work on if you wanted to change the fit of your clothes?
    a. body composition
    b. muscular strength
    c. muscular endurance
    d. flexibility

40. Which of the following choices would be most likely to prevent muscle or joint injury?
    a. activities that alter body composition
    b. activities that increase your CRE
    c. activities that improve your muscular strength and flexibility
    d. eating a balanced diet

41. Which of the following fitness components would you be *least likely* to work on if you wanted to prevent, eliminate, or reduce low-back pain?
    a. cardiorespiratory endurance
    b. muscular strength
    c. muscular endurance
    d. flexibility

42. The full spectrum of physical fitness can be envisioned as:
    a. a synonym of good health
    b. muscular strength
    c. a continuum from low to high fitness
    d. cardiorespiratory endurance

43. Regardless of your age, you should consult a physician if you:
    a. plan to begin an exercise program
    b. have specific health concerns
    c. need exercise information
    d. want to change activities

44. Your activity index is *best* determined by
    a. frequency × activity
    b. intensity × activity
    c. intensity × frequency
    d. intensity × duration × frequency

45. All of the following are directions for the 1.5-mile run-walk test *except*:
    a. warm up prior to taking the test
    b. run at top speed for as long as possible
    c. cool down after the test
    d. avoid strenuous activity on the day of the test

46. The most accurate means of assessing body composition is:
    a. body weight
    b. body mass index
    c. pinch test
    d. underwater weighing

47. If your muscles feel sore a day or two after you go hiking or row a boat, you may need improvement in:
    a. muscular strength
    b. flexibility
    c. muscular endurance
    d. cardiorespiratory endurance

48. Which of the following interpretations of men's body fat percentages is correct?
    a. obesity—35% and higher
    b. obesity—25% and higher
    c. low fat—below 17%
    d. low fat—below 15%

49. Which of the following interpretations of women's body fat percentages is correct?
    a. obesity—35% and higher
    b. obesity—25% and higher
    c. low fat—below 17%
    d. low fat—below 15%

50. Among men, a "very high" trunk flexibility rating is:
    a. above 12 inches
    b. 8-10 inches
    c. above 11 inches
    d. 10-11 inches

51. Among women, a "very high" trunk flexibility rating is:
    a. above 12 inches
    b. 8-10 inches
    c. above 11 inches
    d. 10-11 inches

52. All of the following are examples of tests of muscular endurance *except:*
    a. 60-second sit-ups
    b. pinch test
    c. push-ups
    d. modified push-ups

53. Which pair of physical fitness components needs to be improved to positively affect the body's cholesterol?
    a. muscular strength and muscular endurance
    b. muscular strength and body composition
    c. muscular endurance and body composition
    d. cardiorespiratory fitness and body composition

54. To look trimmer, your exercise regimen should focus on improving:
    a. muscular endurance
    b. cardiorespiratory fitness
    c. body composition
    d. flexibility

ANSWERS TO TRUE/FALSE QUESTIONS

1. true
2. false
3. true
4. true
5. false
6. false
7. true
8. false
9. true
10. false
11. false
12. true
13. false
14. true
15. true
16. true

ANSWERS TO MULTIPLE CHOICE QUESTIONS

17. c
18. d
19. a
20. d
21. b
22. a
23. c
24. a
25. c
26. c
27. b
28. a
29. d
30. a
31. b
32. b
33. c
34. a
35. c

36. c
37. d
38. a
39. a
40. c
41. a
42. c
43. b
44. d
45. b
46. d
47. c
48. b
49. a
50. c
51. a
52. b
53. d
54. c

CHAPTER 2

TRUE/FALSE

1. Progressive overload and specificity are the two principles of sound fitness training.

2. "Train, don't strain" is a good training rule.

3. Speed of running should be your guide during cardiorespiratory exercise.

4. Weight training requires five workouts per week.

5. High-intensity activity is usually of limited duration.

6. The cool-down phase of an aerobic workout should not include stretching.

7. Cool-down is necessary only during extreme heat.

8. Weight training is one of the best forms of aerobic exercise.

9. Muscular endurance is best developed through high repetitions.

10. Muscular strength is best developed through calisthenics.

11. The length of a training program is known as *frequency*.

12. The length of a training program is known as *duration*.

13. Stretching is a useful activity for developing flexibility.

14. The process of hypertrophy occurs rapidly.

15. Atrophy of muscles occurs with disuse.

MULTIPLE CHOICE

16. *Progressive overload* is a term that represents:
    a. excessive physical activity
    b. professional guidance during exercise
    c. an exercise system that is designed primarily to manage medical problems
    d. the adaptation of the body to new demands

17. Which of the following *best* describes a training effect related to participation in a regular exercise program?
    a. a rapid heart rate at rest
    b. an increase in the size and weight of skeletal muscles
    c. continued fatigue for twenty-four hours after exercise
    d. muscle soreness

18. Which of the following training suggestions *best* illustrates the concept of specificity?
    a. jogging to prepare for gymnastics
    b. building arm strength following a heart attack
    c. yoga to increase range of movement and become more limber
    d. lifting heavy weights to lose weight

19. Someone who has been sedentary for an extended period of time and who wishes to begin an exercise program would be best advised to:
    a. select a self-paced activity
    b. select a team sport to promote socialization
    c. select an activity that requires skill and presents a challenge
    d. select jogging as the most effective way to begin

20. Which of the following suggestions would be *best* if you want to increase the intensity of your jogging program?
    a. avoid elevating your heart rate beyond what you are used to
    b. prolong the time that you jog
    c. jog more often
    d. add hills or elevation to your jogging course

21. Which of the following questions would you *least* likely ask yourself if you want to determine whether you are applying the principles of progressive overload?
    a. How hard should I exercise?
    b. How pleasurable is my exercise?
    c. How long should I keep at it in each session?
    d. How often should I exercise?

22. Which of the following should be part of your regular exercise program?
    a. Bouncy stretching should precede each regular exercise session.
    b. Stretching should be avoided once you have completed your exercise session.
    c. Gradually reduce the intensity of your activity at the end of your workout.
    d. Terminate strenuous activity abruptly to avoid nausea or lightheadedness.

23. It is true that with repetition of an activity over a period of time:
    a. the body becomes able to do the same work with less exertion
    b. the muscles atrophy
    c. the resting heart rate increases
    d. the heart muscle decreases in size

24. The positive adaptations your body makes to regular progressive exercise are best known as:
    a. hypertrophy
    b. atrophy
    c. changes
    d. training effects

25. The principle that only those body systems stressed by exercise will benefit by exercise is known as the principle of:
    a. progressive overload
    b. intensity
    c. specificity
    d. frequency

26. Which of the following is the clearest sign that you have overloaded excessively?
    a. a rapid heart rate during activity
    b. rapid breathing immediately following exercise
    c. continued fatigue for 10 minutes after exercise
    d. muscle soreness the day after exercise

27. Which of the following is a proper match of the criteria of progressive overload?
    a. intensity; how long
    b. duration; how long
    c. frequency; specificity
    d. duration; how hard

28. Alternating brief rest periods with bouts of exercise is a training method known as:
    a. interval training
    b. weight training
    c. long slow distance
    d. self-paced activity

29. Progressive overload:
    a. is sudden
    b. needs to be painful
    c. causes adaptation
    d. is often risky

30. Which of the following statements is *false*?
    a. Specificity is a basic principle of sound fitness training.
    b. Cool-down is necessary only during extreme heat.
    c. "Train, don't strain" is a good training rule.
    d. High-intensity activity is usually of limited duration.

31. Cross-training is a process designed to:
    a. develop at least two fitness components
    b. develop more than one fitness component using a single activity
    c. develop a number of fitness components by using a variety of activities
    d. use a number of activities to develop a single fitness component

32. When an exercise program is designed to achieve a particular fitness goal, the training principle that is being applied is referred to as:
    a. intensity
    b. specificity
    c. duration
    d. progressive overload

33. The intensity at which an exercise program is begun should depend on the level of:
    a. muscular strength
    b. muscular endurance
    c. physical fitness
    d. flexibility

34. During aerobic activity, the best guide to how rapidly the workload should be increased is:
    a. the amount of resistance you can use
    b. your heart rate during exercise
    c. the number of repetitions you can manage
    d. your ability to stretch

35. When time for exercise is limited, it can be useful to:
    a. increase frequency
    b. increase duration
    c. decrease duration
    d. increase intensity

36. If exercise intensity is demanding, duration is usually:
    a. unaffected
    b. reduced
    c. increased
    d. prolonged

37. Which of the following fitness components, dependent on consumption of extra calories, may be best achieved with a five- to seven-day frequency?

    a. muscular strength
    b. muscular endurance
    c. body composition
    d. flexibility

38. How long should you spend warming up before exercise?

    a. less than five minutes
    b. more than twenty minutes
    c. warming up isn't necessary
    d. at least ten minutes

39. Muscular strength is best developed by weight training when the following number of repetitions is adhered to:

    a. 6-10
    b. 15-25
    c. 30 or more
    d. 12-15

40. Which of the following is best for developing aerobic fitness?

    a. yoga
    b. weight training
    c. rapid walking
    d. calisthenics

41. Which of the following is best for developing flexibility?

    a. yoga
    b. weight training
    c. rapid walking
    d. calisthenics

42. Which of the following is best for muscular strength?

    a. yoga
    b. weight training
    c. rapid walking
    d. calisthenics

43. During the cool-down period, you can expect your body to return to normal in all of the following ways *except*:

    a. heart rate slows
    b. rate of breathing slows
    c. rate of circulation decreases
    d. blood pressure increases

44. Which of the following is a proper match?

    a. intensity—how hard
    b. duration—how hard
    c. frequency—specificity
    d. intensity—how long

45. Which of the following statements best describes the participation by Americans in high-intensity–high-duration exercise?

    a. almost all
    b. less than 25%
    c. about 25%
    d. a majority

ANSWERS TO TRUE/FALSE QUESTIONS

1. true
2. true
3. false
4. false
5. true
6. false
7. false
8. false
9. true
10. false
11. false
12. true
13. true
14. false
15. true

ANSWERS TO MULTIPLE CHOICE QUESTIONS

16. d
17. b
18. c
19. a
20. d
21. b
22. c
23. a
24. d
25. c
26. d
27. b
28. a
29. c
30. b

31. d
32. b
33. c
34. b
35. d
36. b
37. c
38. d
39. a
40. c
41. a
42. b
43. d
44. a
45. b

CHAPTER 3

TRUE/FALSE

1. Aerobic exercise can help control high blood pressure.

2. Aerobic exercise increases HDL cholesterol.

3. Stroke volume is usually higher in a faster-beating heart.

4. Regular aerobic exercise tends to reduce heart rate recovery time.

5. The faster the heart beats during exercise, the better.

6. Jogging is the best aerobic activity.

7. A cardiorespiratory exercise session consists of three phases.

8. A high percentage of LDL cholesterol may protect your heart.

9. Calories can be used to measure the amount of exercise you are getting.

10. Aerobic exercise requires use of the large muscles such as the legs.

11. Yoga is an example of anaerobic activity.

12. CRE training results in a decrease in the normal stroke volume of the heart.

13. Bicycling may improve cardiorespiratory endurance.

14. Adding fifteen minutes to your jogging workout is an excellent way to increase intensity.

15. Increasing exercise intensity to high levels tends to reduce duration.

16. Activities of long duration even when performed at levels below the EBZ seem to afford cardiorespiratory benefits.

MULTIPLE CHOICE

17. Which of the following statements about aerobic activity is *most* accurate?
    a. Aerobic activity outstrips the ability of the heart and lungs to supply the muscles with oxygen.
    b. Aerobic activity creates an "oxygen debt."
    c. Aerobic activity is best characterized by an all-out, maximum effort.
    d. Aerobic activity is best characterized by a sustained effort, usually for at least 20 minutes in duration.

18. Which of the following is the best example of an anaerobic activity?
    a. running a mile
    b. yoga
    c. long-distance swimming
    d. running a 100-yard dash

19. Which of the following statements about the possible effects of CRE training is true?
    a. It decreases the size of the heart muscle.
    b. It increases the oxygen-carrying capacity of the blood.
    c. It increases the resting blood pressure of those with high blood pressure.
    d. It decreases the normal stroke volume of the heart.

20. Which of the following would be the most typical recommendation from a cardiologist to patients recovering from a heart attack or heart surgery or to those who may be at risk of heart attack?
    a. gradually increase physical activity
    b. begin an exercise program, but avoid aerobic activity
    c. be sedentary
    d. avoid formal, supervised exercise programs

21. The number of times per minute that the average heart contracts at rest is:
    a. 50 beats
    b. 60 beats
    c. 70 beats
    d. 80 beats

22. Which of the following statements is *true*?
    a. Scientific studies conclusively prove that regular exercise prevents heart disease.
    b. Significant scientific studies indicate that regular exercise can reduce some of the risk factors suspected of contributing to coronary heart disease.
    c. An increased stroke volume at rest may contribute to coronary heart disease.
    d. Increased collateral circulation may contribute to coronary heart disease.

23. The predicted maximum heart rate of a 20-year-old is:
    a. 175 beats per minute (BPM)
    b. 190 BPM
    c. 200 BPM
    d. 220 BPM

24. Which of the following activities would be *least likely* to develop CRE?
    a. rope skipping
    b. cycling
    c. softball
    d. jogging

25. Which of the following is the percentage range of your maximum heart rate that determines your Exercise Benefit Zone (EBZ)?
    a. 40% to 60%
    b. 50% to 70%
    c. 60% to 85%
    d. 70% to 85%

26. Your Exercise Benefit Zone (EBZ):
    a. may increase or decrease with age
    b. increases with age
    c. decreases with age
    d. stays the same throughout a lifetime

27. Which of the following choices represents the *best* way to increase the intensity of a jogging program?
    a. add 15 minutes to your jog
    b. jog twice each day
    c. jog at the upper threshold of your EBZ
    d. add another day of jogging

28. The minimum number of minutes per session recommended to achieve CRE benefits is:
    a. 5
    b. 10
    c. 15
    d. 20

29. When taking your pulse to monitor your heart rate, it is advisable to:
    a. use the radial artery method only
    b. use the carotid artery method only
    c. count pulse beats for 60 seconds
    d. avoid excessive pressure when using the carotid artery

30. It is most accurate to state that the blood of well-trained individuals:
    a. contains high protein
    b. has more white cells
    c. has a decreased tendency to clot
    d. contains high levels of cholesterol

31. According to the textbook, the Exercise Benefit Zone of a 20-year-old should be:
    a. 148 beats per minute (BPM) - 180 BPM
    b. 120 BPM - 170 BPM
    c. 150 BPM - 165 BPM
    d. 131 BPM - 161 BPM

32. Studies have shown that injuries from jogging can be reduced if workouts stress:
    a. high intensity and short duration
    b. very low frequency and long duration
    c. daily workouts
    d. low intensity and long duration

33. The *minimum* frequency of aerobic workouts necessary to maintain cardiorespiratory fitness seems to be:
    a. 5 times per week
    b. 6 times per week
    c. about every other day
    d. daily

34. All of the following activities are suitable for the "continuous rhythmic technique" of training *except*:
    a. basketball
    b. jogging
    c. cycling
    d. swimming

35. In high-intensity anaerobic exercise:
    a. fast-twitch muscle fibers are used more extensively
    b. lactic acid is produced more slowly
    c. carbohydrates are used slowly
    d. slow-twitch muscle fibers are used more extensively

36. Which of the following matches is *incorrect*?
    a. lactic acid formation—high-intensity exercise
    b. lactic acid—can serve as an important fuel
    c. carbohydrates—an important fuel
    d. fast-twitch muscle fibers—use oxygen rapidly

37. In the United States, coronary heart disease and its relationship to heart attacks:
    a. is a serious health problem but no longer a major cause of death
    b. is the second leading cause of death
    c. is the greatest single cause of death
    d. is no longer a serious health problem

38. Which of the following statements about heart attack is *incorrect*?
    a. It is the result of a process that begins early in life.
    b. It is clear to experts why some persons suffer a heart attack and others do not.
    c. Atherosclerosis presents one of its major risks.
    d. It is usually caused by a reduction of the blood flow to the heart.

39. All of the following are commonly accepted coronary heart disease risk factors *except*:
    a. race
    b. age and sex
    c. family history
    d. stress

40. All of the following statements about high blood pressure are true *except*:
    a. There is no known cure.
    b. It can be controlled.
    c. It can be measured by an instrument called a stethoscope.
    d. It is high when readings are higher than 120/60.

41. Which of the following statements regarding the treatment of high blood pressure is true?
    a. The reduction of blood pressure needs to be 10 or more to result in a 5% reduction in the risk of a heart attack.
    b. Drugs alone represent the best therapeutic approach.
    c. It cannot be effectively treated if the cause is genetic.
    d. Regular CRE exercise can effectively lower both systolic and diastolic pressure for some.

42. Diastolic blood pressure:
    a. tends to decrease with age
    b. is normal in the 120-to-140 range
    c. is the reading obtained as the heart relaxes
    d. is the period when the pressure is highest

43. Which of the following statements about smoking and CHD is true?
    a. The risk does not increase when combined with high cholesterol readings.
    b. The more one smokes and the stronger the cigarette, the greater the risk.
    c. The risk does not increase when combined with hypertension.
    d. Smoking is not a risk factor for CHD.

44. Research suggests that people who regularly do CRE exercises, when compared to those who don't regularly do CRE exercises, tend to have one of the following:
    a. higher HDL levels
    b. higher LDL levels
    c. an increased tendency for their blood to clot
    d. fewer heart attacks and sudden deaths

45. "High risk" total cholesterol levels are those that are higher than
    a. 180 milligrams
    b. 200 milligrams
    c. 240 milligrams
    d. 260 milligrams

46. Desirable total cholesterol levels for adults is less than:
    a. 160 milligrams
    b. 180 milligrams
    c. 200 milligrams
    d. 220 milligrams

47. Which of the following statements about cholesterol is true?
    a. Low-density lipoproteins (LDL) seem to remove cholesterol from blood vessel walls.
    b. High-density lipoproteins (HDL) cause cholesterol to clog the blood vessels.
    c. Cholesterol is a substance manufactured outside of the body.
    d. Cholesterol is essential to the performance of certain body functions.

48. Which of the following types of fats does the body use to manufacture cholesterol?
    a. saturated
    b. unsaturated
    c. monounsaturated
    d. polyunsaturated

49. Which of the following foods is *least* likely to contain large quantities of cholesterol?
    a. egg yolks
    b. egg whites
    c. whole milk products
    d. meats

50. In the report issued by the National Cholesterol Education Program, it is recommended that dietary fat and cholesterol content be reduced:
    a. only if other risk factors exist
    b. for all Americans over age 2
    c. for all Americans over age 18
    d. only if there is evidence of CHD

51. The current recommendation is that the total fat content of what we eat be reduced to:
    a. 10%
    b. 20%
    c. 30%
    d. 40%

52. Fast-twitch muscle fibers are most used during:
    a. running at top speed
    b. jogging
    c. walking
    d. swimming for distance

53. Slow-twitch muscle fibers play the greater role during:
    a. running at top speed
    b. lifting heavy weights
    c. jogging long distances
    d. gymnastics

54. Which of the following risk factors of coronary heart disease can be controlled by a person's behavior?
    a. age
    b. high blood pressure
    c. heredity
    d. sex of the individual

55. The most common disease of the circulatory system is:
    a. low blood volume
    b. anemia
    c. high plasma levels
    d. hypertension

56. Which of the following statements about the reversal of artery blockage is incorrect?
    a. A special low-fat diet can be effective.
    b. Cholesterol lowering drugs are effective.
    c. Regular exercise and a low-fat, low-cholesterol diet can be effective.
    d. Following your regular lifestyle can result in improvement fifty percent of the time.

57. A complete layoff from a regular exercise program can result in a loss of 50% fitness.
    a. in the first week
    b. in the first two weeks
    c. only after three weeks
    d. only after one month

ANSWERS TO TRUE/FALSE QUESTIONS

1. true
2. true
3. false
4. true
5. false
6. false
7. true
8. false
9. true
10. true
11. false
12. false
13. true
14. false
15. true
16. true

ANSWERS TO MULTIPLE CHOICE QUESTIONS

17. d
18. d
19. b
20. a
21. c
22. b
23. c
24. c
25. c
26. c
27. c
28. d
29. d
30. c
31. b
32. d
33. c
34. a
35. a
36. d
37. c
38. b
39. a
40. d
41. d
42. c
43. b
44. a
45. c
46. b
47. d
48. a
49. b
50. b
51. c
52. a
53. c
54. b
55. d
56. d
57. b

CHAPTER 4

TRUE/FALSE

1. To lose fat on your belly, you must do lots of sit-ups.

2. Only a strict diet is effective in fat reduction.

3. Endurance exercises like jogging and cycling can help control weight.

4. For losing weight, walking can be as effective as running.

5. Skipping breakfast can help in weight loss.

6. Exercise automatically increases the appetite.

7. Most crash diets are based on pseudo-scientific theories.

8. Women tend to have a higher percent of body fat than men.

9. To burn fat, the duration of an activity is more essential than the intensity.

10. When you are trying to lose weight, calories don't count.

11. Muscle weighs more than an equal volume of fat.

12. Crash diets are helpful for permanently controlling weight gain.

13. Aerobic exercise burns calories by exercising the large muscle groups of the body.

14. Wearing a rubber sweatsuit during exercise will help melt the fat off.

15. Regular, moderate exercise rarely results in any increase in appetite.

16. Some individuals may be overweight according to the height-weight chart but not be overfat.

17. Rapid weight loss as a result of a crash diet is usually due to a loss of body fat.

18. Anorexia is a disorder that is related to an extreme fear of weight gain.

19. Individuals suffering from bulimia may gorge themselves and then induce vomiting.

MULTIPLE CHOICE

20. When a fat person loses body fat:
    a. the number of fat cells is reduced
    b. both the number of fat cells and their size are reduced
    c. the size of fat cells is reduced
    d. only fluid is lost

21. One pound of fat is equal to approximately:
    a. 2,500 calories
    b. 3,000 calories
    c. 3,500 calories
    d. 4,000 calories

22. Which one of the following activities would be *least* helpful to someone wishing to alter his or her body composition?
    a. 30 minutes of bowling
    b. 30 minutes of weight training
    c. 30 minutes of basketball
    d. 30 minutes of bicycling

23. It is *true* to state that:
    a. exercise can reduce fat in particular parts of the body
    b. exercising with a rubber suit can melt fat faster
    c. exercise can help a person to gain weight
    d. an active person who stops exercising will find that muscle turns to fat

24. Which of the following statements is true?
    a. All diabetics are obese.
    b. Obesity is another term for being overweight.
    c. Men with over 10% body fat are considered obese.
    d. Women with over 20% body fat are considered obese.

25. If food consumed is equal to the energy used in activity, you are in:
    a. positive calorie balance
    b. negative calorie balance
    c. dynamic calorie balance
    d. neutral calorie balance

26. Which of the following statements about crash diets is true?
    a. They are effective for permanent weight loss.
    b. Most crash diets are based upon poor nutritional information.
    c. The large, immediate loss is fat.
    d. They are never harmful.

27. Most authorities seem to believe that permanent weight loss is best achieved by:
    a. high-protein diets
    b. a combination of diet and aerobic exercise
    c. low-carbohydrate diets
    d. exercise without diet

28. Individuals who exercise three to five times a week for up to half an hour at a time generally experience:
    a. an increase in appetite
    b. little, if any, change in appetite
    c. a decrease in appetite
    d. a need for more protein

29. It is correct to state that exercise will, when combined with a balanced weight reduction diet:
    a. require daily exercise
    b. require a 1,000 calorie diet
    c. lessen the chance of losing fat quickly
    d. lessen the chance of losing lean muscle tissue

30. Muscle-strengthening exercises, such as weight training, change body composition by:
    a. burning large numbers of calories
    b. increasing the proportion of muscle to fat
    c. turning fat into muscle
    d. melting fat

31. For losing fat, the *least* important criterion of progressive overload is:
    a. frequency
    b. duration
    c. intensity
    d. activity

32. Which one of the following types of activities burns the most calories?
    a. resistance exercises
    b. stretching exercises
    c. calisthenics
    d. aerobic exercises

33. Which one of the following can contribute to a weight loss program?
    a. weight training
    b. massage
    c. sauna
    d. wearing a rubber suit during exercise

34. Which of the following statements related to body fat is true?
    a. Exercising a body part will reduce fat only in that area.
    b. A vibrating machine is useful in reducing body fat.
    c. Using a sauna is a good way to melt off body fat.
    d. When you exercise, fat is mobilized from all of the body's fat cells; hence "spot reduction" is a myth.

35. All of the following statements about crash diets are true *except*:
    a. Dramatic initial weight loss is almost entirely attributable to the shedding of excess fat.
    b. Most crash diets are based on ill-considered, half-understood, or pseudo-scientific theories.
    c. Crash diets often result in loss of muscle mass.
    d. Crash diets can be potentially dangerous.

36. Which of the following statements would be most helpful to someone on a weight control program?
    a. The more calories you burn, the more effective your program will be.
    b. The duration of your exercise, if longer than ten minutes, is the most important variable.
    c. The intensity of the exercise is the most important variable.
    d. It is not necessary to exercise within your EBZ.

37. For losing fat, the most important criterion of progressive overload is:
    a. frequency
    b. duration
    c. intensity
    d. activity

38. Which one of the following activities would be best for losing fat?
    a. bowling
    b. calisthenics
    c. walking
    d. archery

39. If a person is in negative calorie balance by 500 calories per day, it is likely that one pound will be lost in:
    a. one month
    b. five days
    c. two weeks
    d. seven days

40. If you add 250 calories to your daily diet for one year, you will gain approximately:

    a. 26 pounds
    b. 52 pounds
    c. 13 pounds
    d. 7 pounds

41. A reasonable weekly weight loss should be about:

    a. 2 pounds
    b. 1 pound
    c. 3 pounds
    d. 5 pounds

42. Which of the following pieces of equipment can be effective for losing fat?

    a. vibrating machine
    b. rubber exercise suit
    c. massage machine
    d. stationary bicycle

43. When you exercise, fat is mobilized from:

    a. all the fat cells in the body
    b. the body part being exercised
    c. the waist and hips
    d. the fat cells in the buttocks

44. When a person becomes sedentary but continues eating as before:

    a. muscle becomes fat
    b. muscle tissue is lost and fat is added
    c. weight is lost
    d. weight is always gained

45. Which of the following nonsport activities is highest in energy expenditure?

    a. weeding
    b. driving a car
    c. shoveling snow
    d. mopping floors

46. Which of the following sedentary activities is highest in energy expenditure?

    a. piano playing
    b. eating
    c. card playing
    d. writing

47. Which of the statements relating to body composition is true?
    a. The heavier the body weight, the more the body fat.
    b. Underwater weighing is a measure of body composition.
    c. Body weight is a reliable measure of body composition.
    d. Clothing size is a measure of body composition.

48. The ideal weight loss program attempts to achieve all of the following *except*:
    a. maintain lean body mass
    b. maintain body water
    c. lose body fat
    d. lose muscle and fat

49. Which of the following activities requires the most energy per minute?
    a. bicycling at 13 miles per hour
    b. aerobic dance
    c. tennis
    d. walking at 4.5 miles per hour

50. Which of the following activities requires the most energy per minute?
    a. swimming at 55 yards per minute
    b. bicycling at 13 miles per hour
    c. running at 5 miles per hour
    d. basketball (vigorous, full court)

51. The minimum requirements of an exercise program for altering body composition and losing weight are:
    a. 60 minutes, five times per week
    b. 20 minutes, twice a week
    c. 30 minutes, three times per week
    d. 10 minutes, six times per week

52. Which of the following statements about the burning of fat in the body is *correct*?
    a. Body fat is the major fat burning tissue in the body.
    b. A gain in muscle tissue in the body slows down the rate at which the body burns fat.
    c. Low-intensity, long-duration exercise can be very effective in burning body fat.
    d. High body metabolism slows down the burning of fat.

ANSWERS TO TRUE/FALSE QUESTIONS

1. false
2. false
3. true
4. true
5. false
6. false
7. true
8. true
9. true
10. false
11. true
12. false
13. true
14. false
15. true
16. true
17. false
18. true
19. true

ANSWERS TO MULTIPLE CHOICE QUESTIONS

20. c
21. c
22. a
23. c
24. b
25. d
26. b
27. b
28. b
29. d
30. b
31. c
32. d
33. a
34. d
35. a
36. a
37. b
38. c
39. d
40. a
41. b
42. d
43. a
44. b
45. c
46. a
47. b
48. d
49. a
50. d
51. c
52. c

CHAPTER 5

TRUE/FALSE

1. To build muscle, you should work out at least three times per week.

2. Weight training makes you muscle bound.

3. Muscles shrink in size without regular exercise.

4. Resistance exercise can help improve sports performance.

5. Sore muscles can be relieved by being stretched.

6. The full squat exercise should be avoided.

7. Higher resistance with fewer repetitions is best for developing strength.

8. Sit-ups should be done with bent knees.

9. Isometric exercise produces movement.

10. Weight training should be done throughout the full range of motion.

11. Weight training slows you down.

12. Hypertrophy is an increase in muscle size.

13. In weight training, light resistance and high repetitions lead to muscular endurance.

14. Yoga is one of the best activities for developing muscular strength.

15. Bouncing stretches are safer than static stretches.

MULTIPLE CHOICE

16. A muscular contraction is triggered by:
    a. a muscle fiber
    b. an impulse from a nerve
    c. a muscle cell
    d. a chemical reaction

17. When the muscle fibers in a particular motor unit contract:
    a. the force exerted varies with the resistance
    b. they contract partially
    c. they contract maximally
    d. they exert minimal force

18. With regard to lifting a heavy weight rather than a light weight, it is correct to state that:
    a. more motor units must contract
    b. each motor unit must exert greater force
    c. only strong motor units contract
    d. all of a muscle's motor units contract

19. When weight training is practiced regularly, muscle fibers tend to:
    a. increase in number
    b. increase in size
    c. wear out
    d. become brittle

20. Which of the following statements regarding types of muscular contraction is true?
    a. Isometric contractions have no effect on muscular strength.
    b. Isotonic contractions can develop strength throughout the range of motion.
    c. Isokinetic contractions usually result in muscle soreness.
    d. Isometric contractions primarily improve flexibility.

21. The advised intensity in weight training to develop muscular strength is:
    a. 6 to 8 repetitions
    b. 15 to 25 repetitions
    c. 12 to 18 repetitions
    d. 20 to 28 repetitions

22. Which of the following systems of weight training is best for someone wishing to develop both muscular strength and endurance?
    a. using the correct weight at 3 to 5 repetitions
    b. using the correct weight at 6 to 8 repetitions
    c. using the correct weight at 8 to 15 repetitions
    d. using the correct weight at 15 to 25 repetitions

23. Which of the following statements about weight training is true?
    a. It means the same as weight lifting.
    b. If used by women, it will always result in large, bulky muscles.
    c. It can be done at almost any age.
    d. It can increase a woman's bust size.

24. Which of the following statements regarding weight training is *false*?
    a. It is an excellent means of developing muscular strength and endurance.
    b. If practiced regularly, it can help protect against athletic injuries.
    c. It can be used in rehabilitation.
    d. It reduces joint flexibility.

25. When lifting something from the floor, it makes good sense to:
    a. keep your knees straight
    b. lift with your back
    c. bend your knees and keep your back straight
    d. lift only with your arms

26. Which of the following activities is generally best for developing muscular strength?
    a. weight training
    b. calisthenics
    c. jogging
    d. cross-country skiing

27. Which of the following exercises may be related to low-back problems and is best avoided?
    a. half-knee bend
    b. bent-knee sit-ups
    c. bent-knee leg-raises
    d. straight-leg sit-ups

28. Which of the following is the competitive sport associated with lifting the heaviest possible weight overhead?
    a. weight training
    b. weight lifting
    c. body building
    d. progressive resistance exercise

29. Which one of the following activities emphasizes flexibility?
    a. bicycling
    b. weight training
    c. yoga
    d. swimming

30. Which of the following is *most likely* to result in flexibility problems?
    a. weight training
    b. yoga
    c. calisthenics
    d. jogging

31. The safest effective type of flexibility training is:
    a. bouncing stretches
    b. calisthenics
    c. static stretching
    d. ballistic movements

32. When a joint is not regularly moved through its complete range of motion:
    a. the muscles atrophy
    b. strength is lost
    c. muscular endurance is lost
    d. muscles become shorter and joints may stiffen

33. Which of the following statements is false?
    a. Improving flexibility may make it possible to more easily improve strength through training.
    b. Training increases the rate at which motor units are activated.
    c. The phenomenon of hypertrophy is a process by which the number of muscle fibers increases.
    d. A decrease in muscle size is referred to as *atrophy*.

34. When a muscle is not used for a long period of time, the change that occurs is known as:
    a. atrophy
    b. hypertrophy
    c. muscle bound
    d. tightness

35. Exercise against an immovable object is known as:
    a. isokinetic
    b. isotonic
    c. isometric
    d. concentric

36. Lifting a weight overhead is known as an:
    a. eccentric contraction
    b. isotonic contraction
    c. isometric contraction
    d. ergometric contraction

37. It is correct to state that the benefits of weight training include:
    a. increasing bust size in women
    b. improvement in marathon running
    c. improvement in sports skills
    d. increasing muscular endurance

38. Calisthenics is less likely than weight training to improve:
    a. flexibility
    b. muscular strength
    c. muscular endurance
    d. aerobic fitness

39. Isokinetic contraction is best described as follows:
    a. exercise against an immovable object
    b. movement through a limited range of motion
    c. negative work
    d. exercise during which the speed of movement is constant while the resistance adjusts to the muscle's ability to exert force

40. A system of weight training requiring 8–15 repetitions may be used to develop:
    a. muscular strength
    b. muscular endurance
    c. both muscular strength and muscular endurance
    d. aerobic fitness

41. When compared to the general population, champion weight lifters and body builders are:
    a. less flexible
    b. more flexible
    c. about equal in flexibility
    d. more muscle bound

42. Movement is orchestrated by the:
    a. flexor muscles
    b. extensor muscles
    c. central nervous system
    d. flexor and extensor muscles

43. Which of the following statements regarding the relationship between muscle and the burning of calories by the body is true?
    a. Adding muscle will reduce the number of calories you burn each day.
    b. For every pound of muscle that you add, you will burn 30 to 50 calories per day.
    c. For every pound of muscle that you add, you will burn 100 to 150 calories per day.
    d. The addition of muscle has no significant effect either way in determining the number of calories that you burn each day.

ANSWERS TO TRUE/FALSE QUESTIONS

1. true
2. false
3. true
4. true
5. true
6. true
7. true
8. true
9. false
10. true
11. false
12. true
13. true
14. false
15. false

ANSWERS TO MULTIPLE CHOICE QUESTIONS

16. b
17. c
18. a
19. b
20. b
21. a
22. c
23. c
24. d
25. c
26. a
27. d
28. b
29. c
30. d
31. c
32. d
33. c
34. a
35. c
36. b
37. d
38. b
39. d
40. c
41. b
42. c
43. b

CHAPTER 6

TRUE/FALSE

1. Interval training calls for alternating a relief interval with exercise.

2. In any of the running models, speed is the most important ingredient.

3. Warm-up should always precede an active workout.

4. The model calisthenic circuit training program requires barbells, dumbbells, and other expensive equipment.

5. To calculate your EBZ for swimming, you must first subtract your age from 205.

6. The model weight training program is designed to develop both muscular strength and endurance.

7. When following the model weight training program, resistance should be increased when you can perform ten repetitions.

8. When lifting weights, you should never hold your breath.

9. None of the entry-level model programs requires more than entry-level skills.

10. Swimming is your best exercise choice for changing body composition.

MULTIPLE CHOICE

11. Which of the following components is *least* likely to be developed by the walking/jogging/running program.
    a. cardiorespiratory endurance
    b. muscular endurance
    c. body composition
    d. flexibility

12. How would you rate the contribution of weight training to the development of CRE?
    a. high
    b. moderate
    c. low
    d. none of the above

13. Which of the following pairings of model programs can best contribute to the development of muscular strength?
    a. calisthenic circuit training and swimming
    b. interval circuit training and weight training
    c. bicycling and swimming
    d. weight training and calisthenic circuit training

14. Until your muscles adjust to jogging, it may be wise to:
    a. exercise at less than your EBZ
    b. exercise only once per week
    c. exercise at a high intensity for short periods
    d. lift weights daily

15. It is good advice to limit your weekly increment in walking or jogging to:
    a. a 20% increase in duration
    b. not more than a 50% increase in duration
    c. a 5% increase in duration
    d. not more than a 10% increase in duration

16. How many trips around the interval circuit training program are recommended to influence the development of cardiorespiratory endurance?
    a. 3
    b. 2
    c. 1
    d. 6

17. When you are able to complete three circuits of the calisthenic circuit training program in 20 minutes, you are ready to:
    a. change the exercises
    b. increase your work description
    c. decrease your work description
    d. begin a running program

18. Inexperienced rope skippers should begin the necessary muscular and CRE adjustment to rope skipping by first completing:
    a. calisthenic circuit training
    b. three weeks of weight training
    c. Model Program 1: walking (starting)
    d. one week of interval circuit training

19. Once you begin a model program, you should stick with it for at least:
    a. one week
    b. three to four weeks
    c. two weeks
    d. six months

20. Which of the following statements regarding running, jogging, and walking is true?
    a. Walking can develop all of the components of fitness.
    b. Jogging can be defined as a pace faster than 8 MPH.
    c. Running is better than walking and jogging.
    d. The longer the exercise, the more calories are burned.

21. The foundation of a sound running program is the technique known as:
    a. long slow distance
    b. interval training
    c. circuit training
    d. fartlek

22. As a non-weight-bearing, non-upright activity, swimming:
    a. is more strenuous than running
    b. evokes a higher heart rate per minute during activity
    c. cannot be guided by heart rate per minute
    d. evokes a lower heart rate per minute during activity

23. Which of the following exercises is included in the model weight training program?
    a. clean-and-jerk
    b. military press
    c. reverse curl
    d. two-hands snatch

24. In weight training, the term for the number of times you perform an exercise is:
    a. sets
    b. resistance
    c. repetitions
    d. load

25. To achieve progress in weight training, it is useful to:
    a. do as many repetitions as possible
    b. work out six times per week
    c. increase the resistance daily
    d. use light weights

26. While long slow distance is steady and logical, fartlek is:
    a. a form of circuit training
    b. long distance sprinting
    c. freewheeling and unpredictable
    d. a form of hurdling

27. Interval circuit training as described in the text is a series of:
    a. nine exercises
    b. eight exercises
    c. ten exercises
    d. twelve exercises

28. All of the following equipment is included in the interval circuit *except*:
    a. barbell
    b. step-up bench
    c. jump rope
    d. stationary bicycle

29. For weight training, the system of progression recommended in the text is known as:
    a. specificity
    b. intensity
    c. temporary failure
    d. duration

30. In planning a weight or circuit training program designed to be *best* for improving muscular endurance, the system of repetitions should be:
    a. 15–25
    b. 6–8
    c. 8–15
    d. 10–12

31. The rest interval in interval circuit training lasts:
    a. 30 seconds
    b. 15 seconds
    c. 10 seconds
    d. 45 seconds

32. The exercise interval in interval circuit training lasts:
    a. 30 seconds
    b. 15 seconds
    c. 10 seconds
    d. 45 seconds

33. Regarding the interval circuit, which of the following pairs is correct?
    a. dumbbells—clean-and-press
    b. slant board—sit-ups
    c. barbell—forward raise
    d. jump rope—twister

34. Circuit training arranges exercises for different muscle groups to follow each other for the purpose of:

    a. providing a unique program
    b. fun
    c. delaying the onset of fatigue
    d. variety

35. When your personal best is 18 push-ups in calisthenics circuit training, your work description should be:

    a. 10
    b. 5
    c. 6
    d. 9

36. Which of the following exercises is included in the text's calisthenics circuit?

    a. bent rowing
    b. bench press
    c. parallel squat
    d. leg raise

37. To be most effective, the basic stretching program should be performed:

    a. three times weekly
    b. daily
    c. five times weekly
    d. when the muscles seem tight

38. Which of the following is *not* a significant benefit of rope skipping?

    a. weight loss
    b. muscular endurance of legs
    c. flexibility
    d. cardiorespiratory fitness

39. How many exercises are contained in the model weight training program?

    a. 11
    b. 10
    c. 9
    d. 8

ANSWERS TO TRUE/FALSE QUESTIONS

1. true
2. false
3. true
4. false
5. true
6. true
7. false
8. true
9. true
10. false

ANSWERS TO MULTIPLE CHOICE QUESTIONS

11. d
12. c
13. b
14. a
15. d
16. a
17. b
18. c
19. b
20. d
21. a
22. d
23. b
24. c
25. a

26. c
27. a
28. d
29. c
30. a
31. b
32. a
33. b
34. c
35. d
36. c
37. b
38. c
39. d

APPENDIX B

TRUE/FALSE

1. Activities that are rated low in fitness prerequisite can usually be safely begun even by relatively sedentary persons who follow routine safety precautions as described in Chapter 1.

2. Activities rated high in developing flexibility are usually best for improving body composition.

3. A self-paced, high-CRE activity should be the mainstay of a CRE exercise program.

4. Body composition is most readily improved through activities rated high in muscular strength.

5. Team sports are competitively paced.

6. Activities like walking, jogging, and running are good choices for maintaining flexiblity.

MULTIPLE CHOICE

7. Activities classified as high in CRE must:
    a. raise the heart rate into the EBZ
    b. maintain the heart rate in the EBZ for at least fifteen minutes
    c. develop flexibility
    d. utilize high resistance

8. To serve as the foundation of a CRE program, an activity must rate high in CRE and must also:
    a. develop muscular strength
    b. be competitively paced
    c. be self-paced
    d. maintain flexibility

9. Reduction in body fat is best influenced by sports and activities rated high in:
    a. CRE
    b. muscular strength
    c. flexibility
    d. muscular endurance

10. The ideal activity for developing muscular strength and endurance is:
    a. swimming
    b. calisthenics
    c. gymnastics
    d. weight training

11. Archery, walking, bicycling, and running have one thing in common:
    a. they develop muscular strength
    b. they develop cardiorespiratory endurance
    c. they are self-paced
    d. they are high in flexibility

12. Which of the following activities is rated high in potential for developing *both* cardiorespiratory endurance and muscular endurance?
    a. fencing
    b. bicycling
    c. yoga
    d. skiing (alpine)

13. For which of the following groups of activities should you keep a record of the calories burned when participating?
    a. aerobic dance, cycling, swimming, jogging
    b. weight training, yoga, golf, gymnastics
    c. bowling, sailing, yoga, archery
    d. archery, diving, weight training, sailing

14. Which of the following activities is rated high in its potential for developing flexibility?
    a. running
    b. bicycling
    c. hiking
    d. weight training

15. Which of the following activities is rated low in fitness prerequisite, thus making the activity suitable for beginners?
    a. basketball
    b. calisthenics circuit training
    c. fencing
    d. handball

16. Which of the following matches of activity and muscular strength is correct?
    a. basketball—high
    b. ballet—low
    c. judo—high
    d. karate—high

17. Which of the following matches of activity and muscular endurance requirement is correct?

    a. lacrosse—moderate
    b. rope skipping—moderate
    c. ultimate frisbee—low
    d. hiking—high

18. Which of the following matches of activity and flexibility is correct?

    a. aerobic dance—high
    b. weight training—high
    c. ballroom dancing—high
    d. bicycling—moderate

ANSWERS TO TRUE/FALSE QUESTIONS

1. true
2. false
3. true
4. false
5. true
6. false

ANSWERS TO MULTIPLE CHOICE QUESTIONS

7. b
8. c
9. a
10. d
11. c
12. b
13. a
14. d
15. b
16. c
17. d
18. a

CHAPTER 7

TRUE/FALSE

1. You are more likely to stick to a fitness program if it is fun, interesting, and consistent with your health, skill, and fitness needs.

2. Your fitness activities should be selected before you can be clear about your fitness goals.

3. To achieve your goals, your choice of activity should be consistent with the principles of progressive overload and specificity.

4. Even with specific health problems, many people can benefit from a regular exercise program.

5. Unless exercise fits easily into your daily schedule, it is unlikely that you will continue your program.

6. Working out with a training partner is always better than working out alone.

7. Appropriate rewards for reaching short-term goals can help you stick with your program.

8. Overzealousness frequently leads to injury.

MULTIPLE CHOICE

9. The first step in getting started on an exercise program, after you have assessed your fitness status, is to:
    a. select activities
    b. set personal goals
    c. sign a contract
    d. buy equipment

10. The most important criterion for selecting activities for your fitness program is that each activity should:
    a. develop muscular strength
    b. require a training partner
    c. match your goals and fitness needs
    d. require no equipment

11. When embarking on a new exercise program, it is wise to:
    a. do as much as you can, as quickly as you can
    b. work hard enough to feel muscle soreness the day after the workout
    c. push for immediate results
    d. start out doing less than you think you can, and progress slowly

12. Which of the following groups of activities is *most* likely to develop cardiorespiratory endurance?
    a. bicycling, walking, and swimming
    b. weight training and stretching
    c. gymnastics and calisthenics
    d. tennis, archery, and alpine skiing

13. If you have been sedentary, it is best to select an aerobic activity that is:
    a. a team sport
    b. self-paced
    c. competitive
    d. high in beginning intensity

14. Which of the following activities is best for developing flexibility?
    a. rope skipping
    b. gymnastics
    c. yoga
    d. jogging

15. Which of the following goal statements can be measured objectively?
    a. having more energy
    b. reducing the resting heart rate
    c. strengthening the immune system
    d. looking sexier

16. All of the following matches of activity with fitness component are correct *except*:
    a. weight training—muscular strength
    b. cross country skiing—aerobic fitness
    c. yoga—flexibility
    d. running—muscular strength

17. All of the following matches of fitness goal with fitness component are correct *except*:
    a. prevent joint injury—aerobic fitness
    b. prevent premature heart attack—aerobic fitness
    c. firm up muscles—muscular strength
    d. prevent joint injury—flexibility

18. Your personal fitness contract should include information about your:
    a. specific weight training exercises
    b. intended frequency and duration
    c. beginning body fat
    d. beginning muscle size

19. All of the following will help you to keep going on your fitness program *except*:
    a. setting aside a special time for exercise
    b. varying your program from time to time
    c. rewarding yourself for reaching minimum goals
    d. never varying your program

ANSWERS TO TRUE/FALSE QUESTIONS

1. true
2. false
3. true
4. true
5. true
6. false
7. true
8. true

ANSWERS TO MULTIPLE CHOICE QUESTIONS

9. b
10. c
11. d
12. a
13. b
14. c
15. b
16. d
17. a
18. b
19. d

CHAPTER 8

TRUE/FALSE

1. A high-protein diet can provide more energy.

2. A steak eaten before working out is the best energy source.

3. Your diet should contain more carbohydrates than protein.

4. Exercisers need greater amounts of vitamins.

5. Eggs are high in cholesterol.

6. Vitamins A, D, E, and K are fat soluble.

7. Starchy foods such as baked potatoes are complex carbohydrates.

8. Beef liver is higher in cholesterol than is lean beef.

9. Polyunsaturated fats tend to lower serum cholesterol.

10. Margarine is as high in saturated fat as is butter.

11. Water is considered to be the most important nutrient.

12. Fats have more calories per unit of weight than do carbohydrates.

13. Carbohydrates are found in animal foods.

14. Cholesterol is made in the body from saturated fats.

15. Vitamin C is water soluble.

16. Authorities are divided on whether vitamin supplements are necessary.

17. Antioxidants are "free radicals" which over time cause damage to cells and cell walls.

MULTIPLE CHOICE

18. Which of the following nutrients are known as the "building blocks" of the body?
    a. minerals
    b. fats
    c. proteins
    d. carbohydrates

19. Most human energy is derived from:
    a. minerals
    b. fats
    c. proteins
    d. carbohydrates

20. Most nutritionists recommend that we eat a greater proportion of unrefined complex carbohydrates for all of the following reasons *except* :
    a. to build body tissue
    b. to spare body protein as an energy source
    c. to allow fats to be used more efficiently
    d. to supply fuel for intensive activity

21. The nutrient which contains twice as much energy as either protein or carbohydrate is:
    a. vitamin C
    b. fat
    c. calcium
    d. iron

22. Which of the following is a water soluble vitamin?
    a. A
    b. D
    c. K
    d. B1

23. A good source of vitamin D is:
    a. sunlight
    b. yellow vegetables
    c. cereals
    d. cauliflower

24. Calcium is important in:
    a. hormone regulation
    b. energy production
    c. bone formation
    d. oxygen transport

25. The "Dietary Goals for the United States" call for increasing the consumption of:
    a. naturally occurring carbohydrates
    b. salt
    c. saturated fats
    d. sugar

26. Which of the following matches related to the "Dietary Goals" is correct?
    a. fat; retain at 42% of total food intake
    b. carbohydrate; decrease to 46% of total food intake
    c. protein; retain at 12% of total food intake
    d. fat; increase saturated fats to 16% of total food intake

27. It is correct to state that:
    a. Whole milk is a better choice than skimmed milk.
    b. Your total calories should not exceed your daily energy needs unless you want to gain weight.
    c. Cheese is low in saturated fats.
    d. Polyunsaturated fats are found primarily in meats.

28. The American Heart Association recommends that dietary cholesterol be limited to not more than 300 mg. per day, because:
    a. cholesterol is constipating
    b. cholesterol is fattening
    c. cholesterol isn't essential to the body
    d. a high level of cholesterol is a risk factor in heart disease

29. Which of the following foods have no cholesterol?
    a. eggs
    b. fruits and vegetables
    c. liver
    d. fish

30. Which of the following is an empty-calorie food?
    a. apples
    b. milk
    c. soft drinks
    d. potatoes

31. Which of the following is the *best* advice to a regular exerciser?
    a. eat a balanced diet
    b. take protein supplements
    c. take vitamin supplements daily
    d. eat fewer carbohydrates

32. A balanced diet can be derived from:
    a. the Scarsdale Diet
    b. the Food Guide Pyramid
    c. the Beverly Hills Diet
    d. rice

33. All of the following functions are fulfilled by nutrients *except*:
    a. providing energy
    b. building and repairing body tissues
    c. regulating body processes
    d. lowering blood pressure

34. Which of the following is a true statement about protein?
    a. Protein is found only in animal foods.
    b. Only animal protein is considered "complete."
    c. Most Americans suffer from a lack of sufficient protein.
    d. Protein supplements are necessary for exercisers.

35. A function of vitamin A is to:
    a. improve blood clotting
    b. regulate calcium absorption
    c. ensure energy metabolism
    d. aid in tooth and bone development

36. The mineral iron is important for:
    a. oxygen transport
    b. fat metabolism
    c. glucose metabolism
    d. formation of body tissues

37. You should limit all of the following *except*:
    a. saturated fat
    b. foods adequate in fiber
    c. sugar
    d. salt

38. It is generally agreed that saturated fat should be eliminated or limited in one's daily diet to:
    a. 10% of total intake
    b. 15% of total intake
    c. 20% of total intake
    d. 25% of total intake

39. The dietary goal for carbohydrate intake is:
    a. 30%
    b. 10%
    c. 12%
    d. 58%

40. The "Food Guide Pyramid" calls for the following match:
    a. fruit-vegetables—four servings daily
    b. bread-cereal—six to eleven servings daily
    c. milk—four to five servings daily
    d. meat, fish, etc.—four to five servings daily

41. Skimmed milk is a better choice than whole milk because:
    a. it tastes better
    b. it is more nourishing
    c. it is lower in fat
    d. it is cheaper

42. Which of the following is a monounsaturated fat?
    a. coconut oil
    b. olive oil
    c. corn oil
    d. soybean oil

43. Which of the following contains the most cholesterol?
    a. ten clams
    b. eight ounces of whole milk
    c. one cup of ice cream
    d. ten small shrimp

44. Suggestions for eating more fiber include all of the following *except*:
    a. reduce your intake of water
    b. eat some fiber at each meal
    c. avoid overcooking
    d. get fiber from a variety of foods

45. Which of the following is a high-fat fish containing omega 3 fatty acids?
    a. snapper
    b. sole
    c. salmon
    d. pike

46. Soluble fiber, such as is found in oat bran and beans, may increase the level of:
    a. cholesterol
    b. HDL
    c. LDL
    d. total fat

47. The best nutritional aid to good health is:
    a. a vitamin supplement
    b. a high-protein diet
    c. a daily mineral supplement
    d. a balanced diet

48. Which of the following does not contain caffeine?
    a. coffee
    b. tea
    c. orange juice
    d. cola

49. Which of the following statements is true?
    a. A high-protein diet provides more energy.
    b. Exercisers need more vitamins.
    c. Margarine is lower in calories than is butter.
    d. Water is the most important nutrient.

50. Current recommendations regarding the intake of fats in the daily diet suggest that the largest quantity of fat should be:
    a. monounsaturated
    b. polyunsaturated
    c. saturated
    d. multisaturated

51. Tropical oils, such as palm, palm kernel, and coconut oil, are largely:
    a. monounsaturated
    b. polyunsaturated
    c. saturated
    d. not useful in manufacturing cholesterol

52. Which of the following statements regarding the intake of high-fiber diets is false?
    a. It is one of the essential nutrients.
    b. It aids the passage of waste through the digestive system.
    c. If fiber intake is increased too quickly, it can cause unpleasant side effects.
    d. They may increase the level of HDL.

53. Which of the following foods would be a poor source of fiber?
    a. oat bran
    b. fruits
    c. eggs
    d. vegetables

54. The statement that best characterizes the position of 50% of Americans regarding the use of vitamin supplements seems to be:
    a. They can be dangerous.
    b. They are not helpful.
    c. They are essential.
    d. Use them—why take a chance.

55. All of the following are tips for cutting back on fat in your diet *except:*
    a. Avoid fried foods.
    b. Snack on chips and nuts.
    c. Snack on fruits and vegetables.
    d. Limit serving sizes of meat, fish, and poultry.

ANSWERS TO TRUE/FALSE QUESTIONS

1. false
2. false
3. true
4. false
5. true
6. true
7. true
8. true
9. true
10. false
11. true
12. true
13. false
14. true
15. true
16. true
17. false

ANSWERS TO MULTIPLE CHOICE QUESTIONS

18. c
19. d
20. a
21. b
22. d
23. a
24. c
25. a
26. c
27. b
28. d
29. b
30. c
31. a
32. b
33. d
34. b
35. d
36. a
37. b
38. a
39. d
40. b
41. c
42. b
43. d
44. a
45. c
46. b
47. d
48. c
49. d
50. a
51. c
52. a
53. c
54. d
55. b

CHAPTER 9

TRUE/FALSE

1. Ideally, your ultimate target weight should be based on a body fat assessment.

2. It is best to try to lose weight as rapidly as possible.

3. Unless your reasons for wanting to lose weight are vitally important to you, you will probably fail.

4. Crash diets generally fail because they are nutritionally flawed and they do not permanently alter your lifelong approach to eating and exercise.

5. According to the model weight loss program, you should eat only when you are hungry.

6. Positive self-talk can help keep you on your weight loss program.

7. Persons with more muscle tend to burn more calories even at rest.

8. It is unhealthy to walk after a meal.

9. Exercise causes the burning of more calories at rest for some time after the actual exercise is over.

10. Eating slowly, taking at least 20 minutes to finish a meal, will usually result in your eating less food.

11. Step 1 in the model weight loss program is to plan your weekly menu in advance.

12. For permanent results, it is best to lose weight slowly and gradually.

13. For weight control, it is best to plan your menus a week ahead of time.

14. Shopping for food should be done when you are hungry, so that you are sure to make the right choices.

15. To be useful for losing weight, calories must be burned only during intensive physical activity.

MULTIPLE CHOICE

16. Which of the following statements is correct?
    a. Crash diets are generally successful for permanent weight control.
    b. The authors of your textbook believe in improving body composition through a plan that includes diet and exercise.
    c. Altering eating behavior is usually a simple matter.
    d. Omitting food from the bread and cereals food group is the safest way to lose body fat.

17. One pound of body fat is equal to the following number of calories:
    a. 3,500
    b. 4,400
    c. 1,750
    d. 2,000

18. According to the meat exchange, one ounce of lean meat should contain calories in the amount of:
    a. 100
    b. 78
    c. 55
    d. 80

19. According to the milk exchange, one serving of milk should contain calories in the amount of:
    a. 100
    b. 78
    c. 55
    d. 80

20. According to the fruit exchange, one serving of fruit should contain calories in the amount of:
    a. 40
    b. 78
    c. 55
    d. 80

21. Maintaining an appropriate negative calorie balance will enable you to:
    a. lose body fat
    b. maintain your present weight
    c. gain weight
    d. lose muscle

22. The best way to stick to your daily food calorie goals is to:
    a. eat out more often
    b. have someone else do the cooking
    c. plan your weekly menus in advance
    d. skip breakfast whenever possible

23. Irregular eating, a major cause of overeating, can be controlled by:
    a. exercising instead of eating
    b. skipping breakfast
    c. eating only when you are ravenous
    d. planning ahead for your three meals and scheduled snacks

24. If you tend to eat huge quantities at mealtimes, you can help prevent this by:
    a. preparing enough food for one portion only, and immediately packing away any additional food for leftovers
    b. snacking only on vegetables
    c. keeping junk foods out of the house
    d. eating only when you are hungry

25. All of the following are good tips for eating out, *except*:
    a. never eat out alone
    b. request that salad dressings and gravies be served on the side
    c. stick to drinking water, diet drinks, or skimmed milk
    d. order broiled or baked foods rather than fried foods

26. Which of the following statements about burning extra calories is *true*?
    a. Walking as a low-intensity activity isn't helpful for weight control.
    b. The greater the duration of the activity, the more calories will be burned.
    c. Routine activities have no role in weight control.
    d. Using stairs instead of elevators has little influence on your weight.

27. The model weight control program has a better chance for success than a crash diet because it:
    a. depends on your eating less food
    b. eliminates all junk food
    c. deals with the habits that caused weight gain in the first place
    d. allows you to eat irregularly

28. Limiting yourself to a few meals per day will:
    a. ensure permanent weight loss for most people
    b. shrink your stomach
    c. burn up only body fat
    d. result in slowed metabolism, thus conserving rather than causing a loss in body fat

29. The "Food Exchange Plan" is designed primarily to provide:
   a. a method for planning nutritionally balanced menus
   b. a list of foods
   c. the calorie content of all foods
   d. a diet that will result in the loss of five pounds per week

30. Which of the following statements is a good tip for managing common eating problems?
   a. Eat irregular meals.
   b. Choose the right foods.
   c. Eat only twice a day.
   d. Eat while watching television.

31. If your eating problem is that you tend to consume large helpings of food, it may help to:
   a. choose only foods you dislike
   b. serve your food on small plates
   c. eat only one meal a day
   d. fast for one day a week

32. To control your weight, you should probably deal with snacking by:
   a. avoiding snacks
   b. eating small portions of ice cream
   c. developing a taste for raw vegetables
   d. eat only at mealtime

33. All of the following are common eating problems *except*:
   a. trigger eating
   b. using food to replace feelings
   c. eating irregular meals
   d. eating socially

34. Which of the following statements about burning calories is true?
   a. Walking has no effect on weight control.
   b. Only aerobic sports and activities can help in weight loss.
   c. Exercise has no effect on weight loss.
   d. Using stairs instead of the elevator can help to control weight.

35. Exercise raises the metabolism in all of the following ways *except* by:
   a. burning more calories during activity
   b. resulting in a higher metabolism after exercise
   c. building muscle tissue, which burns more calories at rest than fat
   d. melting body fat

ANSWERS TO TRUE/FALSE QUESTIONS

1. true
2. false
3. true
4. true
5. false
6. true
7. true
8. false
9. true
10. true
11. false
12. true
13. true
14. false
15. false

ANSWERS TO MULTIPLE CHOICE QUESTIONS

16. b
17. a
18. c
19. d
20. a
21. a
22. c
23. d
24. a
25. a
26. b
27. c
28. d
29. a
30. b
31. b
32. c
33. d
34. d
35. d

CHAPTER 10

TRUE/FALSE

1. During a stress response, blood flow is slowed to hands and feet as protection against excessive bleeding in case of injury.

2. Everyone experiences stress in exactly the same way.

3. Signs of the onset of stress that can be classified as "internal signs" include moist and cold hands, profuse sweating, pounding heart, and upset stomach.

4. The best physical activities for controlling stress are those that can be enjoyed as play.

5. Techniques for reducing stress can be expected to work the first time you try them.

6. Thirty minutes of daily aerobic exercise is an effective strategy to combat stress.

7. Stress and nutrition are totally unrelated.

8. Deep breathing for relaxation is best when you focus on breathing through your abdomen rather than through your chest.

9. A certain amount of stress is useful in improving performance.

10. For most people, competition reduces stress.

MULTIPLE CHOICE

11. Which of the following is generally considered a stress-related change?
    a. blood flow to the hands is increased
    b. blood pressure is reduced
    c. pulse rate is slowed
    d. breathing is rapid and shallow

12. All of the following changes are responses to a stressful situation *except*:
    a. muscles become tense to enhance movement
    b. blood flow increases to the muscles and brain
    c. metabolic rate slows
    d. all the senses become more efficient

13. The kind of stress that induces good health and improved performance is known as:

    a. psyched out
    b. eustress
    c. distress
    d. calmness

14. All of the following are categories of signals of the onset of stress *except*:

    a. mood signs
    b. internal signs
    c. musculoskeletal signs
    d. visual signs

15. To be most beneficial in lowering stress, the physical activities you choose should:

    a. exclude those in which winning and competition are essential ingredients
    b. consist of individual sports only
    c. be passive in nature
    d. include those in which competition is important

16. Exercise can help deal with stress in all of the following ways *except*:

    a. it can burn up the biochemical by-products of stress
    b. it may relieve excessive muscle tension
    c. it can enhance feelings of well-being
    d. it always relaxes your muscles

17. The technique of concentrating on words or objects to become relaxed is known as:

    a. muscle relaxation
    b. mental rehearsal
    c. meditative relaxation
    d. deep breathing

18. Reducing stress by learning to use your time more effectively is a strategy of:

    a. imagery
    b. lifestyle change
    c. planned coping
    d. physical exercise

19. The bodily response to threatening situations is frequently known as:

    a. eustress
    b. distress
    c. the "fight-or-flight" response
    d. the stand up and fight response

20. When stress increases to the point at which health and performance suffer, it is called:
    a. eustress
    b. distress
    c. illness
    d. overexcitement

21. Which of the following is an internal sign of excessive stress?
    a. twitching
    b. stiff neck
    c. worrying
    d. chills

22. Which of the following is a musculoskeletal sign of excessive stress?
    a. twitching
    b. chills
    c. heart flutterings
    d. worrying

23. Whether you fight or run away when attacked, you have responded appropriately and:
    a. your tension will remain high
    b. your increased level of tension will dissipate
    c. your blood pressure will remain high
    d. your distress will remain high

24. According to the Student Stress Scale, the most stressful life event is:
    a. divorce of parents
    b. jail term
    c. being fired from job
    d. death of a close family member

25. As a preventive measure, regular exercise conditions your body so that when stress occurs:
    a. the body doesn't react
    b. muscles don't spasm
    c. recovery is more rapid
    d. tension doesn't occur

26. Mentally rehearsing a stressful scene in which physiological arousal occurs, and then successfully controlling the response, is known as:
    a. imagery
    b. planned coping
    c. meditative relaxation
    d. stress inoculation

ANSWERS TO TRUE/FALSE QUESTIONS

1. true
2. false
3. true
4. true
5. false
6. true
7. false
8. true
9. true
10. false

ANSWERS TO MULTIPLE CHOICE QUESTIONS

11. d
12. c
13. b
14. d
15. a
16. d
17. c
18. c
19. c
20. b
21. d
22. a
23. b
24. d
25. c
26. d

CHAPTER 11

TRUE/FALSE

1. If a club does not request medical clearance, you should not join.

2. If the club lacks such aerobic equipment as stationary bicycles, treadmills, rowing machines, or running space, it will be difficult for you to develop CRE.

3. If a club meets your needs but doesn't provide progress cards, it is wise not to join.

4. If you are interested in a commercial facility to ensure competent guidance in achieving your fitness goals, be sure that an adequate number of qualified instructors will be available at the time that you plan to use the club.

5. Exercise programs that are advertised as "no sweat" are unlikely to help you develop CRE.

MULTIPLE CHOICE

6. Which of the following are negative factors related to health club membership costs?
   a. long-term contracts
   b. high-pressure selling
   c. no credit for enforced absences due to illness or injury
   d. all of the above

7. Which of the following would best assure a well-rounded program in a health club?
   a. resistance exercise machines
   b. free weights
   c. equipment to develop all five fitness components
   d. stationary bicycles

8. The best time to visit a club you are thinking of joining is:
   a. when a salesperson has the time to see you
   b. at the hour at which you plan to use it, to be sure that there is adequate equipment
   c. when it looks its best
   d. after you have made the decision to join

ANSWERS TO TRUE/FALSE QUESTIONS

1. false
2. true
3. false
4. true
5. true

ANSWERS TO MULTIPLE CHOICE QUESTIONS

6. d
7. c
8. b

CHAPTER 12

TRUE/FALSE

1. Health limitations are not necessarily a deterrent to exercise.

2. Most Type 2 (adult onset) diabetics are obese and may benefit from aerobic exercise with a physician's approval.

3. A person with a fractured wrist won't be able to retain cardiorespiratory fitness.

4. If a woman exercised regularly before becoming pregnant, she will have to stop until she gives birth.

5. When lifting a load from the floor, it is wise to use your thighs rather than your back in order to prevent injury.

MULTIPLE CHOICE

6. Before persons with particular health problems begin a new exercise program, they should first:
   a. begin a walking program
   b. consult their physician
   c. select an activity
   d. buy home equipment

7. Persons with hypertension generally do best in programs that focus on:
   a. cardiorespiratory fitness
   b. muscular strength
   c. muscular endurance
   d. flexibility

8. The most common orthopedic complaint in this country is:
   a. tennis elbow
   b. runner's knee
   c. bursitis
   d. low-back pain

9. The Kegel exercise recommended for women is used to strengthen the:
   a. pelvic floor
   b. lower back
   c. abdominals
   d. hips

10. The majority of diabetics are non-insulin dependent, and exercise can help by contributing to all of the following *except*:
    a. the need for less insulin
    b. the loss of body weight
    c. an increase in the body's insulin receptors
    d. for facilitating the action of the body's own insulin

11. Which of the following is *not* a viable purpose of exercise in case of an orthopedic problem?
    a. may substitute for surgery
    b. recondition muscles after surgery
    c. automatically reduces the need for medication
    d. restores range of motion after removal of a cast

12. In case of a lower-back problem, using a lumbar roll can help to:
    a. cure the cause of the problem
    b. make wearing high-heeled shoes more comfortable
    c. replace medication
    d. produce the correct hollow in the lower back

13. Which of the following is consistent with the "RICE" principle of managing acute injuries?
    a. exercise
    b. rest
    c. contact a physician
    d. isolate the injury

14. Which of the following muscle groups *least* affects your back?
    a. muscles along the spine
    b. muscles of the hip
    c. abdominal muscles
    d. shoulder muscles

15. Which exercise should be part of a back-strengthening regimen?
    a. bench press
    b. military press
    c. sit-up
    d. forward raise

ANSWERS TO TRUE/FALSE QUESTIONS

1. true
2. true
3. false
4. false
5. true

ANSWERS TO MULTIPLE CHOICE QUESTIONS

6. b
7. a
8. d
9. a
10. a
11. c
12. d
13. b
14. d
15. c

CHAPTER 13

TRUE/FALSE

1. You generally burn more calories in cold weather than in warm weather.

2. Men and women seem to tolerate exercise in the heat in about the same way.

3. Drinking cold water in the heat causes stomach cramps.

4. Distance runners should run on the balls of the feet to prevent injury.

5. Smokers, on the average, score lower in endurance performance than non-smokers.

6. A sprain should be treated as soon as possible by applying ice while elevating the injured area.

7. Contact sports are inherently more dangerous for women than for men.

8. Many authorities believe that regular exercise seems to delay the onset of so-called age-related problems.

9. Wool and polyester are good insulators in cold weather.

10. Rain wear that doesn't breathe is best to wear for running in the rain.

MULTIPLE CHOICE

11. When exercising outdoors in cold weather, cold, dry air may:
    a. burn your lungs
    b. freeze your blood
    c. cause frostbite in your mouth
    d. feel irritating to your throat

12. The key to dressing for outdoor exercise in cold weather is to:
    a. wear a heavy, down-filled jacket
    b. wear a rubberized sweat suit
    c. dress in layers
    d. wear cotton clothing

13. A waterproof sweat suit worn during exercise may result in:
    a. a greater loss of body fat
    b. dehydration
    c. the melting of fat from the muscles used
    d. the shrinking of fat cells

14. Drinking water during aerobic exercise:
    a. may be necessary to prevent dehydration
    b. impairs performance and should be avoided
    c. causes muscle cramps
    d. upsets the normal activity of the heart

15. Which of the following is a good rule for exercising in hot weather?
    a. Avoid drinking water before beginning exercise.
    b. Take salt pills before prolonged exercise.
    c. Never exercise outdoors in hot weather.
    d. Drink a glass of fluid about ten minutes before aerobic exercise.

16. Cigarette smoking may affect exercise performance by:
    a. limiting the amount of air your lungs can take in
    b. limiting the amount of carbon dioxide your lungs can expel
    c. causing your heart to beat faster
    d. all of the above

17. Once you have achieved your fitness goals, the minimum program required to remain at that level is:
    a. to decrease intensity and frequency but maintain duration
    b. to decrease frequency but maintain intensity and duration
    c. to maintain frequency, duration, and intensity
    d. to decrease duration but maintain frequency and intensity

18. All of the following suggestions may help to prevent shinsplints *except*:
    a. to wear shoes with a raised heel
    b. to avoid running on hard surfaces
    c. to wear well-cushioned shoes
    d. to exercise in bare feet

19. The most important element in preventing frostbite during winter activity is:
    a. heavy exercise
    b. avoidance of drinking cold water
    c. proper clothing
    d. short periods of exercise

20. Which of the following is a *poor* choice for dealing with frostbite?
    a. Cover the spot with a gloved hand.
    b. Rub the area with snow.
    c. Step into a warm room.
    d. Apply warm water indoors.

21. Cross-training may be best described as:
    a. several weight training exercises
    b. weight training plus any other exercise
    c. running plus weight training
    d. a training regimen containing more than one form of exercise

22. Most runners who wear socks prefer those that allow perspiration to escape. Such socks are made of:
    a. orlon
    b. cotton
    c. nylon
    d. a combination of nylon and cotton

23. One advantage of light nylon shorts and shirts is that they:
    a. absorb moisture better than cotton does
    b. are heavier than cotton
    c. can be laundered in the shower
    d. are always cheaper

24. The best way to treat blisters is to:
    a. apply heat
    b. puncture them and let the fluid drain out
    c. apply ice
    d. cut the skin away completely

25. All of the following are common exercise irritation sites *except*:
    a. the crotch
    b. the nipples
    c. the thighs
    d. the elbows

26. Ideally, acute tendinitis should be treated with:
    a. rest and stretching
    b. walking and weight training
    c. light jogging
    d. calisthenics

27. When pain occurs under the kneecap, it is commonly known as:
    a. tight hamstrings
    b. tight quadriceps
    c. pronation
    d. runner's knee

28. The best way to relieve the pain of shinsplints is to:
    a. exercise the muscles to strengthen the shins
    b. elevate the leg, apply ice, and rest
    c. try running uphill
    d. have an orthotic device designed

29. Which of the following statements about women is true?
    a. Exercise should be avoided during menstruation.
    b. Exercise causes cessation of the menstrual cycle.
    c. Vigorous activity causes iron deficiency.
    d. Women can safely participate in contact sports.

30. If you regularly exercise in hot weather and find that you are rapidly losing weight, you are probably:
    a. losing muscle
    b. losing fat
    c. dehydrating
    d. losing muscle and fat

ANSWERS TO TRUE/FALSE QUESTIONS

1. true
2. true
3. false
4. false
5. true
6. true
7. false
8. true
9. true
10. false

ANSWERS TO MULTIPLE CHOICE QUESTIONS

11. d	21. d
12. c	22. a
13. b	23. c
14. a	24. b
15. d	25. d
16. d	26. a
17. b	27. d
18. d	28. b
19. c	29. d
20. b	30. c

TRANSPARENCY MASTERS

CHAPTER 1

1. Physical Fitness
2. Physical Fitness Continuum
3. Do I Need Medical Clearance?
4. How Active Are You?
5. Components of Physical Fitness
6. Fitness Summary
7. Goals and Components

CHAPTER 2

8. Progressive Overload
9. Achieving Progressive Overload
10. Specificity
11. Cross-Training
12. Training Principles

CHAPTER 3

13. Aerobic vs. Anaerobic
14. Specificity for Developing Cardiorespiratory Endurance
15. Cardiorespiratory Training Effects
16. Cardiorespiratory System
17. Coronary Heart Disease Risk Factors
18. Cholesterol, Exercise, and Coronary Heart Disease
19. Exercise Benefit Zone
20. EBZs for Various Ages
21. Taking Your Pulse
22. Computing Your EBZ
23. Progressive Overload for CRE
24. The Aerobic Workout
25. Calorie Guide to CRE

CHAPTER 4

26. Interpreting Body Fat Percentages
27. Calorie Balance
28. Crash Diets
29. Calorie Costs of Selected Fitness Activities
30. Progressive Overload for Body Composition
31. Calorie Costs of Selected Nonsport Activities
32. Calorie Costs of Selected Sedentary Activities

CHAPTER 5

33. Muscular Strength vs. Muscular Endurance
34. Benefits of Muscular Strength and Endurance
35. Law of Use
36. Isotonic vs. Isometric vs. Isokinetic
37. Progressive Overload for Muscular Strength and Muscular Endurance
38. Weight Training: Fact or Myth?
39. Exercises to Avoid
40. Flexibility
41. Progressive Overload for Flexibility

CHAPTER 6

42. Model Programs
43. Calorie Costs for Walking/Jogging/Running
44. Selecting a Program: Walking/Jogging/Running
45. Sample Progressions
46. Interval Circuit Training
47. Exercises for Interval Circuit Training
48. Sample Log for Interval Circuit Training
49. Log for Interval Circuit Training
50. Step-by-Step Guide to Calisthenics Circuit Training
51. Calisthenics Circuit Training Record Card
52. Exercises for Calisthenics Circuit Training
53. Basic Stretching Program
54. Exercises for Basic Stretching Program
55. Warm-up/Cool-down
56. Swimming Programs
57. Calorie Costs for Bicycling and Rope Skipping
58. Exercises for Weight Training Program
59. Weight Training Progress Chart

APPENDIX B

60. Choosing Sports and Activities

CHAPTER 7

61. Fitness Contract
62. Selecting a Sport or Activity
63. Compliance Tips
64. Program Plan
65. CRE Progress Chart

CHAPTER 8

66. Essential Nutrients
67. Dietary Guidelines
68. Dietary Goals
69. Food Guide Pyramid
70. Cholesterol Content of Selected Foods
71. Determining How Much Fat to Consume
72. Calculating Fat Calories from Food

CHAPTER 9

73. Reasons to Lose Weight
74. Weight Loss Goals 1
75. Weight Loss Goals 2
76. Daily Intake Log
77. Daily Output Log
78. Weekly Calorie Balance Form
79. Weight Control Contract
80. Sample Menu Planner
81. Portions and Calories
82. Daily Menu Planner
83. Exercise Tips
84. Weight Control Progress Graph
85. Tips for Managing Eating Problems
86. Things to Keep in Mind in Your Weight Loss Program

CHAPTER 10

87. Fight or Flight
88. Recognizing Distress
89. Personal Stress Scale
90. Managing Stress

CHAPTERS 11, 12, 13

91. Choosing an Exercise Facility
92. Exercises for Low-back Pain
93. Injuries

1 Physical Fitness

The President's Council on Physical Fitness and Sports characterizes physical fitness as the ability to carry out daily tasks without becoming fatigued and with ample energy left to enjoy regular leisure-time pursuits and to handle an occasional unexpected emergency requiring physical exertion. Physical fitness also includes the ability to last, to bear up, and to persevere under difficult circumstances.

2 Physical Fitness Continuum

Low level of fitness ←——————————————→ High level of fitness

1	2	3	4	5	6
Need help to function.	Just able to get around; unfit for work or active leisure.	Tired at end of day; no energy left for active leisure.	Minimum energy left at end of day for active leisure.	Energy left at end of day for wide variety of vigorous activities.	Trained athletes.

Kusinitz/Fine, *Your Guide to Getting Fit*, Third Edition. © 1995 Mayfield Publishing Company

3 Do I Need Medical Clearance?

In general, if you are under 35, have no physical complaints, and have had a medical checkup within the past two years, it is probably safe for you to begin an exercise program at your current level of physical activity and gradually increase it.

Regardless of your age, consult your physician before beginning a fitness program if:

- You are not feeling well.
- You have specific health concerns.
- You experience leg cramps with brisk walking.
- You experience shortness of breath when others don't.
- You are 20 percent over your desirable weight and much of the excess is body fat.
- You have been sedentary for a long time.
- You have a history of any cardiovascular disease.
- You are 35 or older and have a history of any of the following risk factors for coronary heart disease:
- Diabetes
- Hypertension
- High blood cholesterol levels
- A blood relative who had a heart attack before age 60
- Cigarette smoking

4 How Active Are You?

Rating:

Your intensity _____ X your duration _____ X your frequency _____ = your activity index _____.

Assessing your activity index:

Here's how you can translate your activity index into your estimated level of activity:

If your activity index is:	Your estimated level of activity is:
Less than 15	Sedentary
15-24	Low active
25-40	Moderate active
41-60	Active
Over 60	High Active

5 Components of Physical Fitness

Physical fitness component	Definition
Cardiorespiratory endurance	Ability to do moderately strenuous activity over an extended period of time.
Body composition	Percentage of the body that is fat.
Muscular strength	Ability to exert maximum force in a single exertion.
Muscular endurance	Ability to repeat movements over and over or to hold a particular position for a prolonged period.
Flexibility	Ability to move a joint easily through its full range of motion.

6 Fitness Summary

Components of Physical Fitness

Activity index: _____ Estimated level of activity: _____

Components and tests	Results	Rating	Comments
Cardiorespiratory endurance			
Modified step test	_____	_____	_____
1.5-mile run-walk	_____	_____	_____
Body composition			
Percentage body fat	_____	_____	_____
Pinch test (p. 16)	_____	N/A	_____
Mirror test (p. 16)	_____	N/A	_____
BMI	_____	_____	_____
Muscular strength			
Grip strength	_____	_____	_____
Muscular endurance			
60-second sit-up	_____	_____	_____
Push-up	_____	_____	_____
Modified push-up	_____	_____	_____
Flexibility			
Trunk flexibility	_____	_____	_____

Kusinitz/Fine, *Your Guide to Getting Fit*, Third Edition. © 1995 Mayfield Publishing Company

7 Goals and Components

Goals	CRE	Body composition	Muscular strength	Muscular endurance	Flexibility
Increase stamina in such activities as jogging, swimming, dancing, bicycling, long walks	✔	✔		✔	
Increase resistance to muscle fatigue	✔		✔	✔	
Increase muscular effectiveness for daily tasks, sports activities			✔	✔	✔
Become more muscular; firm up muscle tone		✔	✔	✔	
Reduce risk of circulatory and respiratory system disorders	✔	✔			
Lower high blood pressure	✔	✔			
Help to improve control of diabetes	✔	✔			
Lower cholesterol and/or triglyceride levels	✔	✔			
Increase high-density lipoprotein cholesterol	✔	✔			
Reduce discomfort from arthritis		✔			✔
Prevent, eliminate, or reduce muscle and/or joint injury			✔		✔
Decrease muscle soreness due to physical activity				✔	✔
Have more energy at the end of a day's activities	✔			✔	
Improve posture				✔	✔
Reduce menstrual discomfort		✔			✔
Prevent heart attack at an early age	✔	✔			
Lower the resting heart rate	✔				
Reduce asthmatic discomfort during exercise	✔				
Increase range of movement and become more limber					✔
Reduce discomfort from tension					✔
Improve fit of clothes		✔			
Lose or gain weight		✔			
Look trimmer by reducing the girth of waist, hips, thighs, arms		✔			

Kusinitz/Fine, *Your Guide to Getting Fit*, Third Edition. © 1995 Mayfield Publishing Company

8 Progressive Overload

Progressive overload:

The gradual increase of demands on the body systems that cause the body to mobilize its resources and become adapted to the increased workload.

Progressive overload can be achieved by increasing intensity, duration, and/or frequency.

Training effects:

The physiological adaptations resulting from progressive overload.

9 Achieving Progressive Overload

To achieve progressive overload, you must increase one or more of the following factors:

Intensity = How Hard
- Increase the resistance
- Increase the repetitions
- Increase the rate of speed

Duration = How Long
- Increase the time
- Increase the distance
- Increase the number of sets

Frequency = How Often
- Increase the number of workouts

10 Specificity

Your fitness program must be specifically designed to meet your goals. For every fitness goal there are a variety of appropriate activities to choose from.

Select activities based on the principle of specificity: **Only those body systems stressed by an exercise program will benefit from the training.**

11 Cross-Training

You may prefer to alternate two or more activities to improve a single component of fitness. Choosing more than one activity is called **cross-training**.

Sample Cross-Training Program to Improve Cardiorespiratory Endurance:

Day	Activity
Monday	Walk
Tuesday	Bicycle
Wednesday	Walk
Thursday	Swim
Friday	Bicycle
Saturday	Walk
Sunday	Swim

12 Training Principles

Fitness components	Examples of specificity	Progressive overload		
		Intensity	Duration	Frequency
Cardiorespiratory endurance (see Chapter 3)	Bicycling, jogging, rope skipping, swimming, walking	Increase pace as heart rate permits; maintain heart rate in EBZ (see p. 53)	Gradually prolong exercise time; 20 minutes is minimum for training effects	At least every other day
Body composition (see Chapter 4)	Bicycling, jogging, swimming, walking	Increase pace as heart rate permits	Gradually prolong exercise time; 30 minutes is minimum for training effects	At least every other day; aim for 5 days a week if goal is to reduce body fat and/or weight
Muscular strength (see Chapter 5)	Weight training	Use barbells to perform 6 repetitions; at 10 repetitions, increase weight	Increase by repeating each set of 6–10 repetitions	At least every other day
Muscular endurance (see Chapter 5)	Calisthenics	Increase difficulty of exercises	Increase by repeating each set of repetitions	At least every other day
	Weight training	Use barbells to perform 15–25 repetitions; at 25 repetitions, increase weight	Increase by repeating each set of 15–25 repetitions	At least every other day
Flexibility (see Chapter 5)	Calisthenics, modern dance, yoga	Use moderate force to stretch joints	Gradually prolong stretching time for each exercise from 10 up to 60 seconds	At least every other day

Kusinitz/Fine, *Your Guide to Getting Fit*, Third Edition. © 1995 Mayfield Publishing Company

13 Aerobic vs. Anaerobic

The Aerobic Process:

The supply of oxygen keeps pace with the energy demands of the particular activity.

Energy needs increase with the intensity of the activity.

The Anaerobic Process:

When CRE is low or intensity of activity is very high, energy demands outstrip the oxygen supply and fatigue occurs rapidly. After the conclusion of an anaerobic activity, the heart and lungs work overtime.

Jogging is **aerobic**.

Sprinting is **anaerobic**.

14 Specificity for Developing Cardiorespiratory Endurance

Criteria for aerobic activities:

- Meet oxygen demand as you exercise.

- Keep heart rate in exercise benefit zone.

- Use large muscle groups such as legs.

Examples of aerobic activities:

Walking

Jogging

Cycling

Swimming

Rope Skipping

Rowing

Cross-Country Skiing

15 Cardiorespiratory Training Effects

An increase in:

- Size and strength of heart
- Stroke volume
- Cardiac output
- Number of blood vessels
- Blood volume
- HDL cholesterol
- Cardiorespiratory endurance
- Oxygen-carrying capacity

A decrease in:

- Resting heart rate
- Heart rate recovery time
- Blood pressure
- Triglyceride level
- Body fat
- Stress level
- Tendency for blood to clot

16 Cardiorespiratory System

Lung capillaries

Left atrium

Mitral valve

Left ventricle

Interventricular septum

Right ventricle

Tricuspid valve

Inferior vena cava

Right atrium

Superior vena cava

Aorta

Oxygenated blood ⟶
Oxygen-poor blood ⇢

Kusinitz/Fine, *Your Guide to Getting Fit*, Third Edition. © 1995 Mayfield Publishing Company

17 Coronary Heart Disease Risk Factors

The most commonly accepted risk factors for CHD include:

* 1. High blood pressure

* 2. Blood fat abnormalities (high cholesterol, low high-density lipoproteins)

* 3. Smoking

   4. Age and sex

   5. Family history of heart disease

* 6. Physical inactivity

* 7. Diabetes

* 8. Obesity

* 9. Stress

* Can be controlled by lifestyle management.

18 Cholesterol, Exercise, and Coronary Heart Disease

- Cholesterol is an essential fatty-type substance found in some foods and is also manufactured by the body from saturated fats.

- Cholesterol is carried in the blood where it is connected to blood particles called lipoproteins.

- Low-density lipoprotein (LDL) can cause clogging of the lining of the arteries.

- High-density lipoprotein (HDL) protects against clogging by removing cholesterol from the blood.

- HDL levels can be increased by vigorous exercise.

- Decreasing the daily intake of saturated fats can reduce levels of LDL.

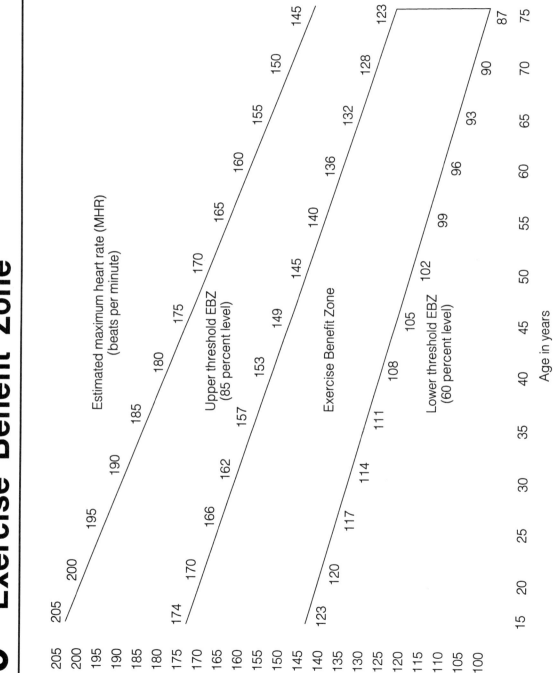

20 EBZs for Various Ages

| | | Exercise Benefit Zone | | | |
| | | 60% estimated MHR | | 85% estimated MHR | |
Age	Estimated MHR per minute	60 sec.	10 sec.	60 sec.	10 sec.
15	205	123	21	174	29
20	200	120	20	170	28
25	195	117	20	166	28
30	190	114	19	162	27
35	185	111	19	157	26
40	180	108	18	153	26
45	175	105	18	149	25
50	170	102	17	145	24
55	165	99	17	140	24
60	160	96	16	136	23
65	155	93	16	132	22
70	150	90	15	128	21
75	145	87	15	123	21

Kusinitz/Fine, *Your Guide to Getting Fit*, Third Edition. © 1995 Mayfield Publishing Company

21 Taking Your Pulse

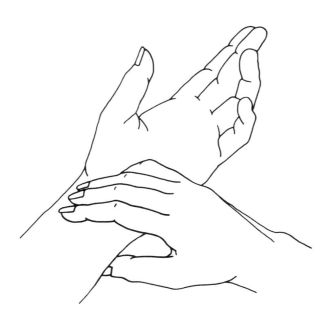

Taking radial pulse

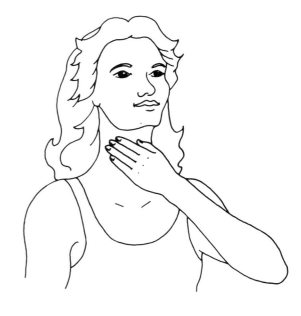

Taking carotid pulse

22 Computing Your EBZ

Predicted maximum HRM = 220 – your age
Your predicted maximum HRM = ____

Minimum EBZ = predicted max HRM x .60
Your minimum EBZ = ____

10-second conversion EBZ (minimum) = EBZ ÷ 6
Your 10-second conversion EBZ (minimum) = ____

Maximum EBZ = predicted max HRM x .85
Your maximum EBZ = ____

10-second conversion EBZ (maximum) = EBZ ÷ 6
Your 10-second conversion EBZ (maximum) = ____

Kusinitz/Fine, *Your Guide to Getting Fit*, Third Edition. © 1995 Mayfield Publishing Company

23 Progressive Overload for CRE

Intensity =   60%-85% of maximum (EBZ) heart rate per minute

Duration =   20 minutes in EBZ (minimum)

Frequency =   3 times per week (minimum)

24 The Aerobic Workout

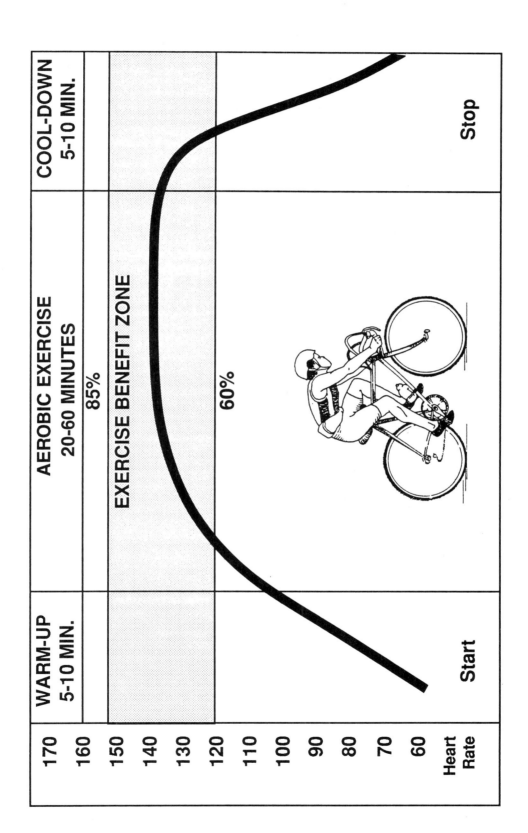

Kusinitz/Fine, *Your Guide to Getting Fit*, Third Edition. © 1995 Mayfield Publishing Company

25 Calorie Guide to CRE

Calories used per week	Duration (minutes per session)	Frequency (days per week)	CRE level
250–500	15–20	3–4	Primarily for beginners with low CRE.
501–750	15–30	3–4	For those who wish to progress from low to moderate levels of CRE.
751–1,250	31–45	3–4	For those who wish to progress from moderate to high levels of CRE.
1,251–2,000	31–45	4–6	To achieve and maintain a very high level of CRE.
Over 2,000	31–60	4–6	To achieve and maintain a very high level of CRE; to try for possible heart-disease prevention benefits.

Kusinitz/Fine, *Your Guide to Getting Fit*, Third Edition. © 1995 Mayfield Publishing Company

26 Interpreting Body Fat Percentages

	Men (%)	Women (%)
Obese	25 and higher	35 and higher
High fat	20-24	30-34
Above average	17-19	25-29
Average	13-16	20-24
Below average	10-12	17-19
Low fat	Below 10	Below 17

Kusinitz/Fine, *Your Guide to Getting Fit*, Third Edition. © 1995 Mayfield Publishing Company

27 Calorie Balance

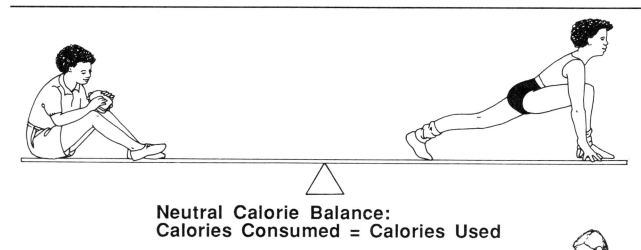

**Neutral Calorie Balance:
Calories Consumed = Calories Used**

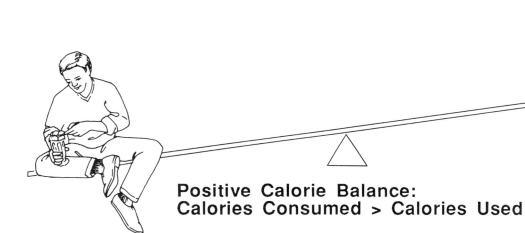

**Positive Calorie Balance:
Calories Consumed > Calories Used**

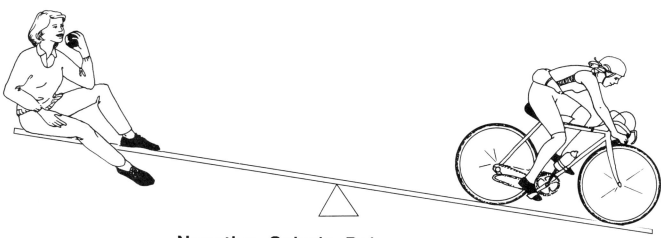

**Negative Calorie Balance:
Calories Consumed < Calories Used**

Kusinitz/Fine, *Your Guide to Getting Fit*, Third Edition. © 1995 Mayfield Publishing Company

28   Crash Diets

Myths About Crash Diets:

- Crash diets will lead to permanent weight loss in a short time.
- Very restricted dieting (for example, only eating fresh fruit or milk products) can be safe and effective.
- Fasting is the most powerful strategy to use in taking off pounds.
- Skipping meals helps lose weight.

Remember the Facts:

- Crash diets are too drastic and difficult to sustain.
- Crash diets frequently lead to health problems.
- High-protein diets may cause excessive fluid loss.
- Muscle tissue is lost in crash diets.

To lose fat, a gradual, long-term program is most effective:

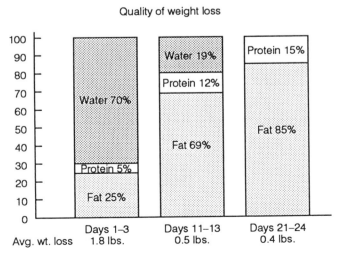

Kusinitz/Fine, *Your Guide to Getting Fit*, Third Edition. © 1995 Mayfield Publishing Company

29 Calorie Costs of Selected Fitness Activities

Activity	Cal./min./lb.	× body weight	× min.	= Activity cal.
Aerobic dance (vigorous)	.062			
Basketball (vigorous, full court)	.097			
Bicycling (13 mph)	.071			
Canoeing (flat water, 4 mph)	.045			
Cross-country skiing (8 mph)	.104			
Handball (skilled, singles)	.078			
Horseback riding (trot)	.052			
Jogging (5 mph)	.060			
Rowing (vigorous)	.097			
Running (8 mph)	.104			
Soccer (vigorous)	.097			
Swimming (55 yds./min.)	.088			
Table tennis (skilled)	.045			
Tennis (beginner)	.032			
Walking (4.5 mph)	.048			
Other (from App. B or Model Programs)				
Other				
Other				
Total per week				

Rating: Estimated calories you expend in fitness activities per week: _____.

30 Progressive Overload for Body Composition

Intensity = Exercise in EBZ

Duration = At least 30 minutes

Frequency = At least 3 times per week (5-7 times per week is better)

Duration and frequency are most important.

31 Calorie Costs of Selected Nonsport Activities

Activity	Cal./min./lb.	× body weight	× min.	= Activity cal.
Bathing, dressing, undressing	.021			
Bed-making (and stripping)	.031			
Chopping wood	.049			
Cleaning windows	.024			
Driving a car	.020			
Gardening				
Digging	.062			
Hedging	.034			
Raking	.024			
Weeding	.038			
Ironing	.029			
Kneading dough	.023			
Laundry (taking out and hanging)	.027			
Mopping floors	.024			
Painting house (outside)	.034			
Plastering walls	.023			
Sawing wood (crosscut saw)	.058			
Shoveling snow	.052			
Other (estimate from above)				
Other				
Other				
Total per week				

Rating: Estimated calories you expend in nonsport activities per week: _____

32 Calorie Costs of Selected Sedentary Activities

Activity	Cal./min./lb.	× body weight	× min.	= Activity cal.
Card playing	.012			
Eating (sitting)	.011			
Knitting and sewing	.011			
Piano playing	.018			
Sitting quietly	.009			
Sleeping and resting	.008			
Standing quietly	.012			
Typing (electric)	.013			
Writing	.013			
Other (estimate additional sedentary activities guided by the above list)	____			
Other	____			
Other	____			
Total per week				

Rating: Estimated calories you expend in sedentary activities per week: _____.

33   Muscular Strength vs. Muscular Endurance

Muscular Strength:

The ability to exert maximum force, usually in a single exertion.

Muscular Endurance:

The ability to repeat movements over and over or to hold a particular position for a prolonged period.

34 Benefits of Muscular Strength and Endurance

- Trim appearance

- Increase in muscle

- Protection against muscle injuries

- Reduction or prevention of low-back problems

- Reduction of bone and muscle loss associated with aging

- Improved sports performance

- Improved mobility

- Less muscle soreness

- Improved posture

- Improved ability to perform daily tasks

35 Law of Use

Each muscle is composed of numerous individual muscle fibers. The number of individual muscle fibers you have does not change over your lifetime. The individual muscle fibers can change in size, depending on how you use your muscles. The more you use a particular muscle, the larger and stronger its individual muscle fibers become.

Hypertrophy:

The harder a muscle works, the larger it becomes.

Atrophy:

When unused, a muscle shrinks in size.

36 Isotonic vs. Isometric vs. Isokinetic

Isotonic Exercise:

- Builds strength through complete range of motion.
- Requires free weights or machines.
- Promotes flexibility when performed correctly.
- Allows easy monitoring of progress.
- Allows sports movements to be performed against resistance.

Isometric Exercise:

- Develops strength only at point of contraction.
- May interfere with blood flow.
- Allows easy monitoring of progress.
- Requires little equipment.

Isokinetic Exercise:

- Develops strength throughout range of motion.
- Requires no negative work, hence less soreness.
- Allows selection of movement speed.
- Requires expensive equipment not readily available.

37 Progressive Overload for Muscular Strength and Muscular Endurance

Intensity:

Goal	Range of repetitions
Muscular strength	6-8
Muscular endurance	15-25
Combination of strength and endurance	8-15

Duration:

To increase or decrease duration, adjust the number of sets and/or the number of exercises.

Frequency:

Every other day is recommended.

38 Weight Training: Fact or Myth?

- Women should not weight train if they wish to avoid overmuscularization.

- Weight training has little use in programs designed to change body composition.

- Weight training should be avoided until one reaches adulthood and once one reaches age 50 or 60.

- Weight training can increase bust size.

- Calisthenics are generally more useful for developing muscular endurance than muscular strength.

39 Exercises to Avoid

Full Squat

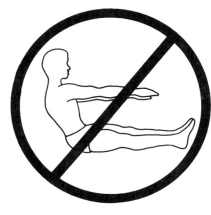

Straight-leg Sit-up

Straight-knee Toe Touch

Plow

Hurdler's Stretch

Also:
- extreme back arches
- any exercise that causes pain

40 Flexibility

Flexibility:

The ability to flex and extend each joint through its normal range of motion.

Benefits:

- Improves mobility

- Reduces muscle soreness

- Helps protect against sports injuries

- Improves posture

- Makes some routine tasks easier

41 Progressive Overload for Flexibility

Intensity = Hold maximum stretch (moderate force)

Duration = Gradually prolong stretching time (10–60 seconds)

Do more than one exercise for each joint

Frequency = 3 to 7 days per week

42 Model Programs

Components of Physical Fitness

Model program	Cardio-respiratory endurance	Body composition	Muscular strength*	Muscular endurance*	Flexibility*
Walking/jogging/running	H	H	M	H	L
Interval circuit training	H	H	H	H	M
Calisthenic circuit training	H	H	M	H	M
Stretching (warm-up/cool-down)	L	L	L	L	H
Bicycling	H	H	M	H	M
Rope skipping	H	H	M	H	L
Swimming	H	M	M	H	M
Weight training	L	M	H	H	H

*Ratings for these components are based on benefits for the specific muscle groups used during the activity in question. (See description of exercises for these model programs in this chapter to identify the muscle groups benefited.) For all other muscle groups, the rating would be low (L).

Kusinitz/Fine, *Your Guide to Getting Fit*, Third Edition. © 1995 Mayfield Publishing Company

43 Calorie Costs for Walking/Jogging/Running

	Speed		
Activity	Miles per hour	Minutes: seconds per mile	Calories per minute per pound
Walking			
Slow	2.0	30:00	.020
	2.5	24:00	.023
Moderate	3.0	20:00	.026
	3.5	17:08	.029
Fast	4.0	15:00	.037
	4.5	13:20	.048
Jogging			
Slow	5.0	12:00	.060
	5.5	11:00	.074
Moderate	6.0	10:00	.081
	6.7	9:00	.088
Fast	7.0	8:35	.092
	7.5	8:00	.099
Running			
Slow	8.5	7:00	.111
Moderate	9.0	6:40	.116
Fast	10.0	6:00	.129
	11.0	5:30	.141

Kusinitz/Fine, *Your Guide to Getting Fit*, Third Edition. © 1995 Mayfield Publishing Company

44 Selecting a Program: Walking/Jogging/Running

Model program 1: walking (starting)

Choose this program if *any* of the following apply:
  You have medical restrictions.
  You are recovering from illness or surgery.
  You tire easily after short walks.
  You are 50 pounds or more overweight.
  You have a sedentary lifestyle.
And if you want to prepare for the advanced walking program (see below) to improve CRE, body composition, and muscular endurance.

Model program 2: walking (advanced)

Choose this program if:
  You already can walk comfortably for 30 minutes.
And if you want to develop and maintain cardiorespiratory fitness, a lean body, and muscular endurance.

Model program 3: walking/jogging (starting)

Choose this program if:
  You already can walk comfortably for 30 minutes.
And if you want to prepare for the jogging/running program (see below) to improve CRE, body composition, and muscular endurance.

Model program 4: jogging/running

Choose this program if both of the following apply:
  You already can jog comfortably without muscular discomfort.
  You already can jog for 15 minutes within your EBZ without stopping or for 30 minutes with brief walking intervals.
And if you want to develop and maintain a high level of cardiorespiratory fitness, a lean body, and muscular endurance.

Model program 5: running (racing)

Choose this program if *all* the following apply:
  You already can jog/run comfortably within your EBZ for 30 to 60 minutes.
  You have been jogging/running regularly for at least 3 months.
  You have had a stress test (if you are among those for whom one is recommended—see pp. 4–5).
And if you want to train for road races as a way of maintaining a high level of cardiorespiratory fitness, a lean body, and muscular endurance.

45 Sample Progressions

Sample Walking/Jogging Progression by Time

Walk interval (seconds)	Jog interval (minutes: seconds)	Number of sets	Total distance (miles)	Total time (minutes: seconds)
:60	:30	10–15	1.0–1.7	15:00–22:30
:60	:60	8–13	1.2–2.0	16:00–26:00
:60	2:00	5–19	1.3–2.3	15:00–27:00
:60	3:00	5–7	1.6–2.4	16:00–28:00
:60	4:00	3–6	1.5–2.7	15:00–30:00

Sample Walking/Jogging Progression by Distance

Walk interval (yards)	Jog interval (yards)	Number of sets	Total distance (miles)	Total time (minutes: seconds)
110	55	11–21	1.0–2.0	15:00–28:12
110	110	16	2.0	26:56
110	220	11	2.0	26:02
110	330	8	2.0	24:24
110	440	7	2.2	26:05
110	440	8	2.5	29:49

46 Interval Circuit Training

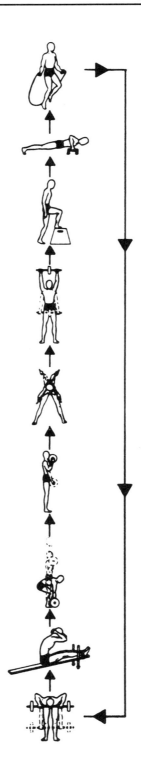

9 ROPE SKIPPING

8 PUSH-UP

7 STEP-UP

6 FORWARD RAISE

5 TWISTER

4 CURL

3 CLEAN AND PRESS

2 SIT-UP

1 ROWING MOTION

47 Exercises for Interval Circuit Training

1. Bent Rowing   2. Sit-up   3. Clean and Press

4. Curl   5. Twister

  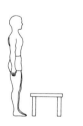  

6. Forward Raise   7. Step-up

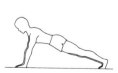 

8. Push-up   9. Rope Skipping

Kusinitz/Fine, *Your Guide to Getting Fit*, Third Edition. © 1995 Mayfield Publishing Company

48 Sample Log for Interval Circuit Training

Exercise		First week	Second week	Third week			
1. Bent rowing	1. 2. 3.	20	20 21	20 + wt. 16 18			
2. Sit-up	1. 2. 3.	18	19 17	18 16 17			
3. Clean and press	1. 2. 3.	17	17 18	18 16 18			
4. Curl	1. 2. 3.	25	26 + wt. 26	24 25 24			
5. Twister	1. 2. 3.	45	50 48	45 40 40			
6. Forward raise	1. 2. 3.	18	20 19	19 16 18			
7. Step-up	1. 2. 3.	20	19 20	19 17 19			
8. Push-up	1. 2. 3.	13	12 10	14 12 12			
9. Rope skipping	1. 2. 3.	25	35 31	35 30 35			

49 Log for Interval Circuit Training

Name _____

Exercise		First week	Second week	Third week			
1. Bent rowing	1. 2. 3.						
2. Sit-up	1. 2. 3.						
3. Clean and press	1. 2. 3.						
4. Curl	1. 2. 3.						
5. Twister	1. 2. 3.						
6. Forward raise	1. 2. 3.						
7. Step-up	1. 2. 3.						
8. Push-up	1. 2. 3.						
9. Rope skipping	1. 2. 3.						

50 Step-by-Step Guide to Calisthenics Circuit Training

1. Learn the twelve exercises described on pp. 126–130. Be able to smoothly perform each exercise in consecutive repetitions.

2. Perform as many arm circles as you can in 30 seconds. Write this number of repetitions in the first max column on the "Calisthenics Circuit Training Record Card." Write half of this number in the work description column labeled "1/2 max."

3. Perform as many jumping jacks as you can in one minute. Write this number of repetitions in the first max column. Write half of this number in the 1/2 max column.

4. Repeat instruction 3 for push-ups, then parallel squats, sit-ups, side leg raises, knees-to-chest, alternate toe touches, squat thrusts, shoulder bridges, and side bends. Rest fully between exercises to obtain true maximums.

5. Run in place at the fastest pace you can for three minutes, counting alternate steps (every left or right). Write this number of repetitions in the max column. Write half of this number in the 1/2 max column.

6. The 1/2 max column should now be completely filled. You now no longer have to worry about timing the individual exercises.

7. When you are ready to begin calisthenics circuit training, note the time you begin on a clock.

8. Perform the twelve exercises in order, each for the number of repetitions you have written in the 1/2 max column. (Remember, time no longer matters for each exercise—just work steadily.) Do not rest between the different exercises.

9. When you have completed all twelve exercises at the 1/2 max number of repetitions (this is one circuit), do two more circuits for a total of three. Do not rest between the circuits.

10. Note the time at the end of the third circuit. Write the date and the total time the three circiuts have taken in the columns labeled "time" and "date" on the record card.

11. When you can perform the three circuits in 20 minutes, increase the number of repetitions (the work description) of each exercise by 1/4 of the present work description. Write this new number in the next work description column.

12. Use the second set of max and time columns to retest yourself after a period of time has elapsed.

51 Calisthenics Circuit Training Record Card

Name _____

Exercise	Max	Time	Max	Time	Work Description					
					1/2 Max					
1. Arm circles		30 sec.		30 sec.						
2. Jumping jacks		1 min.		1 min.						
3. Push-ups		1 min.		1 min.						
4. Parallel squat		1 min.		1 min.						
5. Sit-ups		1 min.		1 min.						
6. Side leg raises		1 min.		1 min.						
7. Knee-to-chest		1 min.		1 min.						
8. Alternate toe touch		1 min.		1 min.						
9. Squat thrust		1 min.		1 min.						
10. Shoulder bridge		1 min.		1 min.						
11. Side bend		1 min.		1 min.						
12. Run in place		3 min.		3 min.						

	Time	Date
1		
2		
3		
4		
5		
6		
7		
8		
9		
10		
11		
12		

	Time	Date
13		
14		
15		
16		
17		
18		
19		
20		
21		
22		
23		

Kusinitz/Fine, *Your Guide to Getting Fit*, Third Edition. © 1995 Mayfield Publishing Company

52 Exercises for Calisthenics Circuit Training

   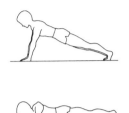 

1. Arm Circles 2. Jumping Jack 3. Push-up 4. Parallel Squat

   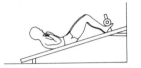

5. Sit-up

6. Side Leg Raise 7. Knee-to-chest

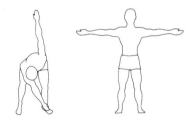 

8. Alternate Toe Touch 9. Squat Thrust

10. Shoulder Bridge

Also: Running in Place 11. Side Bend

Kusinitz/Fine, *Your Guide to Getting Fit*, Third Edition. © 1995 Mayfield Publishing Company

53   Basic Stretching Program

Use static stretching: stretch as far as possible without any repetitive bouncing movements.

Intensity and Duration:

1. Adjustment Phase

   - Let body get used to the position by moving gently into the stretching position.
   - Allow your body to relax and enjoy the melting away of the tight feeling.
   - Hold for 10 seconds; increase to 30 seconds over a period of time.
   - No exertion should be felt in the adjustment phase.

2. Development Phase

   - Repeat the exercise, but stretch a bit farther.
   - Relax and focus on your muscles; feel the stretch without pain.
   - Hold for 15 seconds; as you progress, aim for 60 seconds.

Frequency: Daily

54 Exercises for Basic Stretching Program

1. Shoulder Blade Scratch
2. Towel Stretch
3. Alternate Knee-to-chest

4. Double Knee-to-chest
5. Sole Stretch
6. Seated Toe Touch

7. Seated Foot-over-knee Twist
8. Prone Knee Flexion

9. Wall Lean
10. Stride Stretch

Kusinitz/Fine, *Your Guide to Getting Fit*, Third Edition. © 1995 Mayfield Publishing Company

55 Warm-up/Cool-down

1. Alternate Knee-to-chest 2. Leg Cross-overs 3. Double Knee-to-chest

4. Sole Stretch 5. Seated Toe Touch 6. Sit-up

7. Seated Foot-over-knee Twist 8. Cat Stretch on Knees

 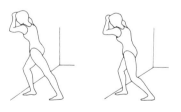

9. Prone Knee Flexion 10. Wall Lean

56 Swimming Programs

As a non-weight-bearing, nonupright activity, swimming evokes a lower heart rate per minute during activity. Therefore, intensity should be guided by an adjusted exercise benefit zone. To calculate your EBZ for swimming, use this formula:

Maximum swimming heart rate (SHR) = 205 − age

Max. SHR X .60 = lower threshold of EBZ

Max. SHR X .85 = upper threshold of EBZ

Determining Calorie Cost for Swimming

Calories per minute per pound	Distance in yards					
	25	100	150	250	500	750
.033	1:15	5:00	7:30	12:30	25:00	30:30
.041	1:00	4:00	6:00	10:00	20:00	30:00
.049	0:50	3:20	5:00	8:20	18:40	25:00
.057	0:43	2:52	4:18	7:10	17:20	21:30
.065	0:37.5	2:30	3:45	6:15	10:00	
.073	0:33	2:13	3:20	5:30	8:50	
.081	0:30	2:00	3:00	5:00	8:00	
.090	0:27	1:48	2:42	4:30	7:12	
.097	0:25	1:40	2:30	4:10	6:30	

57 Calorie Costs for Bicycling and Rope Skipping

Distance (in miles)	Time (in minutes)											
	5	10	15	20	25	30	35	40	45	50	55	60
.50	.032											
1.00	.062	.032										
1.50		.042	.032									
2.00		.062	.039	.032								
3.00			.062	.042	.036	.032						
4.00				.062	.044	.039	.035	.032				
5.00				.097	.062	.045	.041	.037	.035	.032		
6.00					.088	.062	.047	.042	.039	.036	.034	.032
7.00						.081	.062	.049	.043	.040	.038	.036
8.00							.078	.062	.050	.044	.041	.039
9.00								.076	.062	.051	.045	.042
10.00								.097	.074	.062	.051	.045
11.00									.093	.073	.062	.052
12.00										.088	.072	.062
13.00											.084	.071
14.00												.081
15.00												.097

Skipping interval (minutes: seconds)	Rest interval (minutes: seconds)	Number of sets	Total skipping time (in minutes)	Approximate calories used per pound
0:15	0:30	4–10	1–2.5	.07–.18
0:30	0:30	5–10	2.5–6	.18–.43
0:45	0:30	8–12	6–8	.43–.57
0:60	0:30	6–12	8–12	.57–.86
1:30	0:30	8–10	12–15	.86–1.1
2:00	0:60	8	16	1.2
3:00	0:60	6	18	1.3
6:00	1:30	3	18	1.3
9:00	1:30	2	18	1.3
12:00	2:00	2	24	1.7
15:00	0:00	1	15	1.1

Kusinitz/Fine, *Your Guide to Getting Fit*, Third Edition. © 1995 Mayfield Publishing Company

58 Exercises for Weight Training Program

   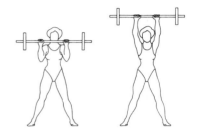

1. Clean and Press 2. Curl 3. Military Press

4. Bent Rowing 5. Bent Arm Pullover and Press 6. Parallel Squat

7. Raise on Toes 8. Sit-up

59 Weight Training Progress Chart

WORKOUT CARD FOR _____

Exercise/Date																				
	Wt.																			
	Sets																			
	Reps																			
	Wt.																			
	Sets																			
	Reps																			
	Wt.																			
	Sets																			
	Reps																			
	Wt.																			
	Sets																			
	Reps																			
	Wt.																			
	Sets																			
	Reps																			
	Wt.																			
	Sets																			
	Reps																			
	Wt.																			
	Sets																			
	Reps																			

Kusinitz/Fine, *Your Guide to Getting Fit*, Third Edition. © 1995 Mayfield Publishing Company

60 Choosing Sports and Activities

RATINGS:

FOR FITNESS COMPONENTS: H = HIGH   M = MODERATE   L = LOW
(IN TERMS OF THE ACTIVITY'S ABILITY TO DEVELOP EACH COMPONENT)

FOR SKILL LEVEL: H = HIGH   M = AVERAGE   L = LOW
(IN TERMS OF THE SKILL LEVEL REQUIRED TO OBTAIN FITNESS BENEFITS)

FOR FITNESS PREREQUISITE: H = SUBSTANTIAL FITNESS REQUIRED
M = SOME PRECONDITIONING REQUIRED   L = NO PREREQUISITE

FOR HOW PACED: 1 = SELF-PACED   2 = COMBINATION OF SELF AND OTHER
3 = PACED BY SOMEONE OTHER THAN YOURSELF

Sports and activities	Components					Skill level	Fitness prerequisite	How paced
	CRE	BC	MS	ME	F			
Aerobic dance	H	H	M	H	H	L	L	3
Basketball	H	H	M	H	M	M	M	2
Bicycling	H	H	M	H	M	M	L	1
Cross-country skiing	H	H	M	H	M	M	M	1
Football/touch	M	M	M	M	M	M	M	2
Frisbee/ultimate	H	H	M	H	M	M	M	2
Hiking	H	H	M	H	L	L	M	1
Jogging and running	H	H	M	H	L	L	L	1
Outdoor fitness trails	H	H	M	H	M	L	L	1
Popular dancing	M	M	L	M	M	M	L	3
Rope skipping	H	H	M	H	L	M	M	1
Sailing	L	L	L	M	L	M	L	1
Skiing/alpine	M	M	H	H	M	H	M	1
Soccer	H	H	M	H	M	M	M	2
Swimming	H	H	M	H	M	M	L	1
Volleyball	M	M	L	M	M	M	M	2
Walking	H	H	L	M	L	L	L	1
Weight training	L	M	H	H	H	L	L	1

61 Fitness Contract

I, _____, am contracting with myself to follow an exercise program to achieve and work at the following fitness goals and components.

Fitness Goals
(Note as many as appropriate.)

Fitness Components
(Check as appropriate.)

	CRE	BC	MS	ME	F
1. _____					
2. _____					
3. _____					
4. _____					
5. _____					
6. _____					
7. _____					
8. _____					

Program Plan

Activities	Components (Check ✓)					Intensity	Duration	Frequency (Check ✓)						
	CRE*	BC*	MS	ME	F			M.	Tu.	W.	Th.	F.	Sa.	Su.
1. _____														
2. _____														
3. _____														
4. _____														
5. _____														
6. _____														
7. _____														
8. _____														
9. _____														
10. _____														

I will begin my program on _____ .

I agree to maintain a record of my activity, assess my progress periodically, and, if necessary, revise my goals.

Signed _____ Date _____

Witness _____

*You should conduct activities for achieving CRE and body composition goals at an intensity within your EBZ.

Kusinitz/Fine, *Your Guide to Getting Fit*, Third Edition. © 1995 Mayfield Publishing Company

62 Selecting a Sport or Activity

- Fun and interest

- Your goals and fitness needs

- Health

- Skill and fitness

- Age

- Time and convenience

- Cost

- Social aspects

63 Compliance Tips

- Progress gradually

- Make exercise an unconditional part of schedule

- Avoid boredom

- Vary the program

- Provide rewards for progress

64 Program Plan

Name _____ Date _____

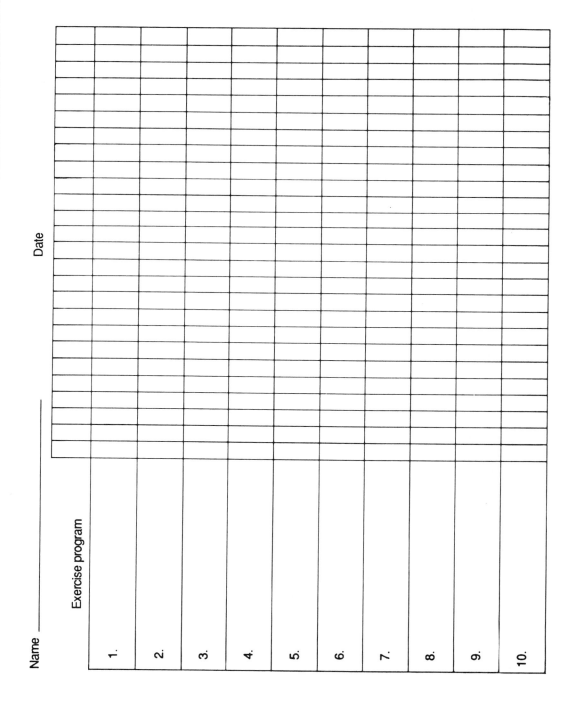

Kusinitz/Fine, *Your Guide to Getting Fit*, Third Edition. © 1995 Mayfield Publishing Company

65 CRE Progress Chart

Week	Activities	Mon.	Tues.	Wed.	Thur.	Fri.	Sat.	Sun.	Weekly distance or time	Weekly calorie cost
1	Walking	30 min.		30 min.		30 min.		30 min.	2 hrs.	468
2	Walking		30 min.	30 min.	30 min.		30 min.	30 min.	2 hrs. 30 min.	585
3	Walk/jog		35 min.	35 min.		35 min.		35 min.	2 hrs. 20 min.	882
4										
5										
6										
7										
8										
9										
10										
11										

66 Essential Nutrients

Nutrient	Function	Major Sources
Protein	Repairs tissue; regulates internal water and acid-base balance; helps in growth, energy	Meat, poultry, fish, eggs, milk and milk products, dry beans, peas, and nuts
Carbohydrates	Main source of energy	Grains, fruits, and vegetables
Fats	Energy, medium for fat-soluble vitamins; excess energy is stored as fat	Saturated fat—from animal foods; Unsaturated fat—from grains, fruits, and vegetables
Vitamins	Act with enzymes to promote the rate of chemical reactions in the body	Abundant in fruits, vegetables, and grains; also found in meat and dairy products
Minerals	Necessary for proper functioning of various body systems	Found in most food groups
Water	Medium for chemical reactions, transport of chemicals	Fruits, vegetables, and other liquids

67 Dietary Guidelines

1. Eat a variety of foods.

2. Avoid excessive fat, saturated fat, and cholesterol.

3. Maintain ideal weight.

4. Eat foods adequate in starch and fiber.

5. Avoid too much sugar.

6. Avoid too much salt and sodium.

7. If you drink alcohol, do so in moderation.

68 Dietary Goals

	Current diet	Dietary goals
Fat	42%	30%
Saturated	16%	10%
Monounsaturated	13%	10%
Polyunsaturated	13%	10%
Carbohydrates	46%	58%
Simple	24%	10%
Complex	22%	48%
Protein	12%	12%

Kusinitz/Fine, *Your Guide to Getting Fit*, Third Edition. © 1995 Mayfield Publishing Company

69 Food Guide Pyramid

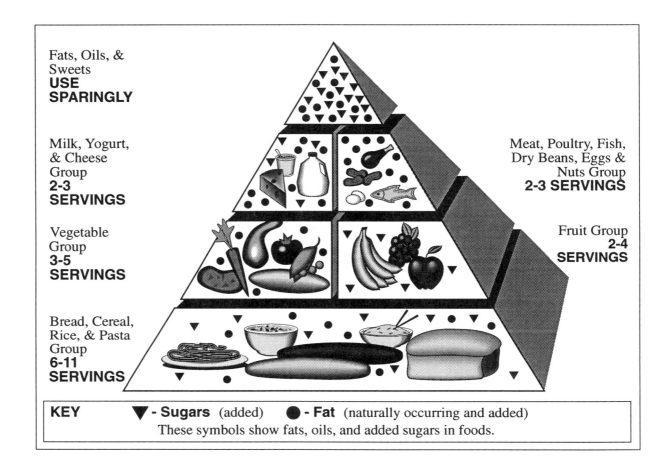

70 Cholesterol Content of Selected Foods

Meat, fish, and eggs	Mg.	Milk and milk products	Mg.
Liver (cooked, 3-1/2 oz.)	438	Milk, whole (8 oz.)	34
Eggs (1 large)	252	Milk, skim (8 oz.)	5
Shrimp (10 small)	150	Cheese, American (1 oz.)	28
Lobster (3-1/2 oz.)	85	Ice cream (1 cup)	85
Clams (10)	60	Ice milk (1 cup)	10
Veal (3-1/2 oz.)	99	Butter (1 pat)	12
Pork (3-1/2 oz.)	88	Cream cheese (1 tbsp.)	18
Beef (3-1/2 oz.)	91	Cottage cheese (4 oz.)	11-24
Lamb (3-1/2 oz.)	100	Yogurt (1/2 cup)	8
Fish (3-1/2 oz.)	50-60	Whipping cream (1 tbsp.)	20
Chicken (3-1/2 oz.)	87	Cheese, Gouda (1 oz.)	21

No more than 300 mg. recommended per day.

Kusinitz/Fine, *Your Guide to Getting Fit*, Third Edition. © 1995 Mayfield Publishing Company

71 Determining How Much Fat to Consume

(Assuming 30% calories from fat)

STEP 1 - Figure out the total number of calories that you consume daily

STEP 2 - Multiply the total number of calories by .30

STEP 3 - Divide the result by 9 (the number of calories in one gram of fat)

EXAMPLE:

Mary Lou consumes about 2,200 calories daily.

2,200 x .30 = 660 calories (from fat) ÷ 9 = 73

(If you are aiming for 20% of your calories from fat, simply use 20% in your calculations instead of 30%.)

72 Calculating Fat Calories from Food

Read the label on the package. If the food serving contains a total of 200 calories and 8 grams of fat, the calculation would be as follows:

1. Multiply the number of fat grams in a serving by 9 (all fats contain 9 calories).

2. In this case the serving contains 8 grams so the equation is:

    8 x 9 = 72 (fat calories in the serving)

3. Divide the number of fat calories by the total number of calories in the serving:

    72 ÷ 200 = 0.36

4. Multiply the answer by 100 as follows:

    0.36 x 100 = 36

5. A serving of food in this example gets 36% of its calories from fat.

73 Reasons to Lose Weight

Importance		*Priority*
_____	Follow my doctor's advice	_____
_____	Wear a smaller clothing size	_____
_____	Improve my appearance	_____
_____	Feel more assured and attractive	_____
_____	Feel healthier and more in control of myself	_____
_____	Firm up muscle tone	_____
_____	Improve sports performance	_____
_____	Please someone who is important to me	_____
_____	Help reduce low-back pain	_____
_____	Lower high blood pressure	_____
_____	Lower cholesterol and/or triglyceride levels	_____
_____	Increase high-density lipoprotein cholesterol	_____
_____	Help control diabetes	_____
_____	Save more energy and increase stamina	_____
_____	Reduce risk of circulatory disease	_____

74 Weight Loss Goals 1

Identifying Weight-Loss and Negative-Calorie-Balance Goals (When Percentage of Body Fat Is Known)

1. $\dfrac{}{\text{\% body fat to be lost}} = \dfrac{}{\text{\% current body fat}} - \dfrac{}{\text{Target \% body fat}}$

2. $\dfrac{}{\text{Pounds to lose}} = \dfrac{}{\text{\% body fat to be lost}} \times \dfrac{}{\text{Current weight}}$

3. $\dfrac{}{\text{Target body weight}} = \dfrac{}{\text{Current weight}} - \dfrac{}{\text{Pounds to lose}}$

4. $\dfrac{}{\text{Number of weeks to achieve target weight}} = \dfrac{}{\text{Total pounds to lose}} \div \dfrac{}{\text{Pounds to lose each week}}$

5. $\dfrac{}{\text{Negative-calorie balance to achieve each week}} = \dfrac{}{\text{Pounds to lose each week}} \times 3{,}500$

Kusinitz/Fine, *Your Guide to Getting Fit*, Third Edition. © 1995 Mayfield Publishing Company

75 Weight Loss Goals 2

Identifying Weight-Loss and Negative-Calorie-Balance Goals (Using Height-Weight Tables)

1. $\dfrac{}{\text{Pounds to lose}} = \dfrac{}{\text{Current weight}} - \dfrac{}{\substack{\text{Target weight (charts,}\\ \text{p. 270}}}$

2. $\dfrac{}{\substack{\text{Number of weeks to}\\ \text{achieve target weight}}} = \dfrac{}{\text{Total pounds to lose}} \div \dfrac{}{\text{Pounds to lose each week}}$

3. $\dfrac{}{\substack{\text{Negative-calorie balance}\\ \text{to achieve each week}}} = \dfrac{}{\text{Pounds to lose each week}} \times 3{,}500$

Kusinitz/Fine, *Your Guide to Getting Fit*, Third Edition. © 1995 Mayfield Publishing Company

76 Daily Intake Log

1 Time	2 Food	3 Amount	4 Calories	5 Comments

Total calorie intake: _____ .

77 Daily Output Log

1 Activity	2 Cal./min./lb.	×	3 Total minutes	×	4 Body weight	=	5 Output
1.		×		×		=	
2.		×		×		=	
3.		×		×		=	
4.		×		×		=	
5.							
6.							
7.							
8.							
Sedentary	.01	×		×		=	

Total calorie output: _____.

Kusinitz/Fine, *Your Guide to Getting Fit*, Third Edition. © 1995 Mayfield Publishing Company

78 Weekly Calorie Balance Form

	Sun.	Mon.	Tues.	Wed.	Thurs.	Fri.	Sat.
Calories in							
Calories out							
Daily difference							
Weekly difference							

79 Weight Control Contract

I, _____, am contracting with myself to follow a weight control program of exercise and diet management to help me alter my body composition.

The body composition goals that I expect to achieve are:

1. _____

2. _____

3. _____

4. _____

5. _____

I expect to achieve a target weight of _____ lbs. by the target date of _____.

During this time, my weekly negative-calorie-balance goal is _____ calories.

My diet plan will include a daily food intake of _____ calories.

My exercise plan will include a daily output of _____ calories.

Physical Activity Plan

Activities*	Session duration	M.	Tu.	W.	Th.	F.	Sa.	Su.
1.								
2.								
3.								
4.								
5.								
6.								
7.								

(Frequency (Check ✓))

I will begin my program on _____.

I agree to maintain a record of my progress, and, if necessary, revise my goals.

Signed _____ Date _____

Witnessed by _____

*Conduct all activities at an intensity within the EBZ, although brisk walking and similar aerobic activities provide greatest calorie-burning effects as a result of durations of more than 30 minutes to over an hour, five times per week.

80 Sample Menu Planner

Date __9/16/87__   Calories per day __1,800__

Meal and Food Group		Portions	Menus
Breakfast	meat	1	½ grapefruit
	fat	1	1 poached egg
	bread	1	1 slice whole wheat toast, 1 tsp. diet margarine
	milk	0	tea or coffee
	veg.	0	
	fruit	1	
Snack	fat	0	1 glass skim milk
	bread	1	2 graham crackers
	milk	1	1 apple
	veg.	0	
	fruit	1	
Lunch	meat	2	4 oz. orange juice
	fat	1	2 oz. turkey on rye bread, tomato, lettuce,
	bread	2	and 1 tsp. mayonnaise
	milk	0	tea or coffee
	veg.	2	
	fruit	1	
Snack	fat	1	1 cup unflavored, low-fat yogurt
	bread	0	2 T. raisins
	milk	1	
	veg.	0	
	fruit	1	
Dinner	meat	4	4 oz. broiled flounder with ½ c. brown rice
	fat	2	½ c. broccoli, ½ c. carrots, sliced tomato
	bread	2	1 slice whole wheat bread with 1 tsp. margarine
	milk	0	¼ cantaloupe
	veg.	3	caffeine-free diet soda
	fruit	1	
Snack	fat	0	3 cups popcorn
	bread	1	celery
	milk	1	1 glass skim milk
	veg.	1	
	fruit	0	

Portions allowed each day: Meat __7__ Fat __5__ Bread __7__ Milk __3__ Veg. __6__ Fruit __5__

Kusinitz/Fine, *Your Guide to Getting Fit*, Third Edition. © 1995 Mayfield Publishing Company

81 Portions and Calories

Portions Allowed from Each Food Group by Calorie Plan

Calorie Plan	Meat	Fat	Bread	Milk	Vegetable	Fruit	Miscellaneous
1,000	3	3	3	2	4	3	—
1,200	6	3	4	2	5	3	1
1,500	7	4	5	3	5	4	2
1,800	7	5	7	3	6	5	2
2,100	9	6	8	4	7	5	2

Calories per Portion

Food group	Portion size	Calories
Meat exchange		
Lean meat	1 ounce	55
Medium-fat meat	1 ounce	78 (omit ½ fat exchange)
High-fat meat	1 ounce	100 (omit 1 fat exchange)
Fat exchange	*	45
Bread exchange	*	70
Milk exchange	*	80
Vegetable exchange		
Group A	½ cup	25
Group B	*	25
Fruit exchange	*	40
Miscellaneous exchange	*	50 (try to avoid; no nutritional value)
Free foods	*	0
Bonus foods	*	110–210 (limit to two times per week)

*See Appendix C, "Food Exchange Plan," for size of portion.

82 Daily Menu Planner

Date _____   Calories per day _____

Meal and Food Group		Portions	Menus
Breakfast	meat fat bread milk veg. fruit		
Snack	fat bread milk veg. fruit		
Lunch	meat fat bread milk veg. fruit		
Snack	fat bread milk veg. fruit		
Dinner	meat fat bread milk veg. fruit		
Snack	fat bread milk veg. fruit		

Portions allowed each day: Meat _____ Fat _____ Bread _____ Milk _____ Veg. _____ Fruit _____

Kusinitz/Fine, *Your Guide to Getting Fit*, Third Edition. © 1995 Mayfield Publishing Company

83 Exercise Tips

Burn more calories routinely:

- No more elevators or escalators—use stairs only.
- Park at the end of parking lots—walk farther to your destinations.
- Do some sort of exercise while you watch TV.
- Whenever possible, walk instead of ride.
- Whenever possible, use manual tools and instruments instead of power tools.
- Pace instead of standing; stand instead of sitting; sit instead of lying down.
- During the work or school day, find a way to climb some stairs every hour or two.

Plan regular exercise periods each day:

- Walking, jogging, cycling, cross-country skiing, rowing, and swimming are the big calorie burners. Done for a long period, hacky-sak will burn calories at the rate of moderate aerobic dance.
- The greater the duration of the activity, the more calories you will burn.
- Incorporate activities to develop muscular strength and muscular endurance activity—more muscle means a higher basic metabolism. This means that you will burn more calories at all times, even while resting.
- Weights, weight machines, the exercise wheel, push-ups, sit-ups, and so on, all build muscle.

84 Weight Control Progress Graph

Starting Weight: _____

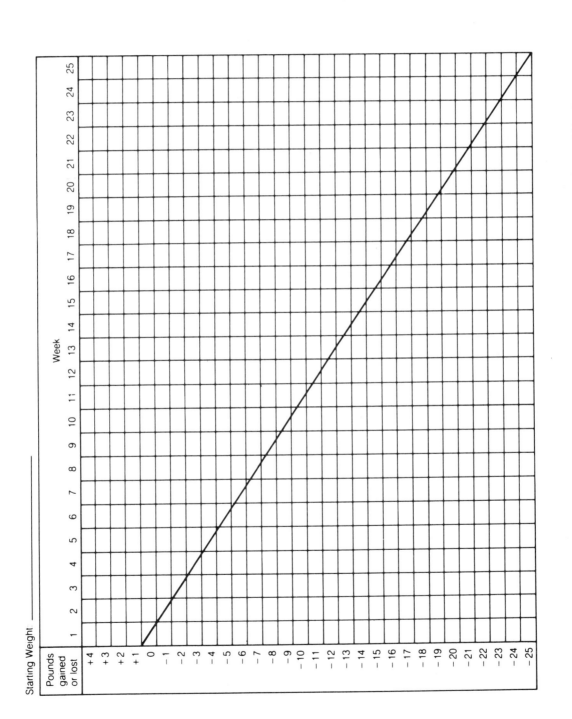

Kusinitz/Fine, *Your Guide to Getting Fit*, Third Edition. © 1995 Mayfield Publishing Company

85 Tips for Managing Eating Problems

- Eat regular meals and planned snacks.
- Choose the right foods.
- Limit the amounts of food you take in.
- Change environmental cues that trigger eating.
- Avoid using food to replace feelings.
- Avoid buying and storing troublesome foods.
- Make wise choices when eating out.

Kusinitz/Fine, *Your Guide to Getting Fit*, Third Edition. © 1995 Mayfield Publishing Company

86 Things to Keep in Mind in Your Weight Loss Program

- It is essential that you eat breakfast and all meals, including snacks, daily.
- You are trying to become inefficient at storing body fat while at the same time becoming efficient at removing or burning body fat.
- When you limit yourself to a few meals per day, your body responds by slowing your metabolism and thus improves its ability to conserve energy and store fat. This is the opposite of what you want to accomplish.
- Whenever possible, walk after a meal to burn fat while it is still in the bloodstream and before it reaches the fat storage cells.
- It takes the appetite control center about 20 minutes to receive the message that you have eaten enough. Therefore, eat slowly; use a teaspoon instead of a tablespoon; chew each mouthful of food ten or more times before swallowing; put the fork or spoon down between each mouthful.
- Dieting without exercise usually leads to a lowered resting metabolism, which makes it harder and harder to lose fat by limiting your food.
- Exercise raises the metabolism in three ways:
  - It causes the body to require more calories during activity.
  - It causes the burning of more calories at rest for some time after the actual exercise is over.
  - It builds muscle, which burns more calories at rest than fat does.
- This system for losing fat and thus reducing weight is specifically designed to be slow and gradual. It has a better chance for lasting success than any crash diet does. It changes or alters the habits that caused weight gain in the first place.

87 Fight or Flight

Sudden and dramatic physiological changes take place to help you survive an extreme threat. These changes are designed to help you fight off the danger or escape from it:

- Your heart rate becomes faster, thus pumping blood more quickly. The faster pace meets your muscles' increased demands for oxygen and nutrients and also dissipates waste products more quickly.
- Your blood pressure rises with the increase in your heart rate.
- Your breathing becomes rapid and shallow.
- Hormones such as epinephrine (adrenaline) pour into your bloodstream.
- All your senses become more efficient.
- Your liver secretes sugar into your blood to meet increased energy needs.
- Your muscles become tense to enhance movement.
- The flow of blood increases to your muscles and brain.
- Blood flow to your digestive organs is restricted.
- Blood flow is slowed to your hands and feet as protection against excessive bleeding in case of injury.
- Your perspiration increases for improved cooling to overcome the heat generated by your increased metabolic rate.

88 Recognizing Distress

Mood signs

I feel "jumpy."

I have trouble sleeping at night.

I worry.

I respond with more anger than necessary.

I feel insecure.

Internal signs

My hands feel moist and cold.

I sweat profusely.

I feel my heart pounding.

My stomach becomes upset.

Musculoskeletal signs

My jaw muscles get tight.

I have frequent headaches.

My muscles feel tense.

My neck becomes stiff.

I develop twitches.

Source: Adapted from Daniel Girdano and George Everly, *Controlling Stress and Tension: A Holistic Approach* (Englewood Cliffs, N.J.: Prentice-Hall, 1979)

89 Personal Stress Scale

To determine *your* stress score, add up the number of points corresponding to the events you have experienced in the past six months or are likely to experience in the next six months.

	Past	Future			Past	Future
1. Death of a close family member	100	☐	17. Increased workload at school	37	☐	☐
2. Death of a close friend	73	☐	18. Outstanding personal achievement	36	☐	☐
3. Divorce between parents	65	☐	19. First quarter/semester in college	35	☐	☐
4. Jail term	63	☐	20. Change in living conditions	31	☐	☐
5. Major personal injury or illness	63	☐	21. Serious argument with instructor	30	☐	☐
6. Marriage	58	☐	22. Lower grades than expected	29	☐	☐
7. Fired from job	50	☐	23. Change in sleeping habits	29	☐	☐
8. Failed important course	47	☐	24. Change in social activities	29	☐	☐
9. Change in health of a family member	45	☐	25. Change in eating habits	28	☐	☐
10. Pregnancy	45	☐	26. Chronic car trouble	26	☐	☐
11. Sex problems	44	☐	27. Change in number of family get-togethers	26	☐	☐
12. Serious argument with close friend	40	☐	28. Too many missed classes	25	☐	☐
13. Change in financial status	39	☐	29. Change of college	24	☐	☐
14. Change of major	39	☐	30. Dropped more than one class	23	☐	☐
15. Trouble with parents	39	☐	31. Minor traffic violations	20	☐	☐
16. New girl- or boyfriend	38	☐	Total			

SOURCE: Adapted from T. H. Holmes and R. H. Rahe, The social readjustment rating scale, *Journal of Psychosomatic Research* 11:213, 1967.

90 Managing Stress

Strategy 1: Relaxation Skills
- Deep breathing: Slow rhythmic breathing to induce a relaxed state
- Progressive muscle relaxation: Skill at recognizing the relaxed state and in inducing muscle relaxation
- Meditative relaxation: Concentrating on words or objects to become relaxed

Strategy 2: Imagery
- Relaxing through visualization: Imagining relaxing scenes that you can trigger in times of stress
- Mental rehearsal: Mentally rehearsing a scene in which you cope effectively with a stressor
- Stress inoculation: Mentally rehearsing a stressful scene that arouses a physiological response that is followed by your successfully controlling the response

Strategy 3: Planned Coping
- Anticipating situations that might cause you stress and implementing a concrete plan for preventing or reducing that stress

Strategy 4: Physical Exercise
- Planning at least 30 minutes a day of regular exercise, preferably aerobic activity

Strategy 5: Lifestyle Change
- Improving your health through adequate nutrition, rest, and exercise
- Preventing or reducing stress by slowing down or learning to use your time more effectively
- Developing supportive relationships such as by joining a group

91 Choosing an Exercise Facility

- Is medical information and clearance requested?
- Is parking adequate?
- Is the staff qualified?
- Can all fitness components be developed?
- Is equipment sufficient so that there is no waiting even at peak hours?
- Are time limitations imposed?
- Is there a system for evaluating progress?
- Are enough instructors available?
- Is the location convenient?
- Are there enough activities to hold your interest over a period of time?
- Can the facility design a program for your special medical needs?
- Does the facility meet industry standards?

92 Exercises for Low-back Pain

1. Alternate Knee-to-chest

2. Leg Crossovers

3. Double Knee-to-chest

4. Sit-up

5. Back Extension

6. Alternate Hip Extension

93 Injuries

Prevention

- Stay in condition; don't exercise sporadically.
- Warm up thoroughly before exercise.
- Use proper body mechanics when lifting objects or executing sports skills.
- Use proper equipment.
- Don't exercise when you are ill, overstrained, or injured.

First Aid for Minor Injuries (R-I-C-E)

Rest: Stop using the injured area as soon as you experience pain.

Ice: Apply ice to the injured area immediately for 15-20 minutes and several times a day for 48 hours after the injury occurs (or until the swelling disappears).

Compression: Wrap the injured body part with an elastic or compression bandage to minimize swelling.

Elevation: Raise the injured part above heart level to decrease the blood supply to the injured area.

Medical Attention

Get medical attention for head and eye injuries, possible ligament injuries, broken bones, and internal disorders such as chest pain, fainting, and heat intolerance. Injuries that don't heal within a reasonable amount of time should also get medical attention.